Mastering Android Application Development

Take your Android knowledge to the next level with this advanced Android application guide, which shows you how to make even better Android apps that users will love

Antonio Pachón Ruiz

open source
community experience distilled

BIRMINGHAM - MUMBAI

Mastering Android Application Development

First published: October 2015

Production reference: 1231015

Published by Packt Publishing Ltd.
Livery Place
35 Livery Street
Birmingham B3 2PB, UK.

ISBN 978-1-78588-422-1

www.packtpub.com

Credits

Author
Antonio Pachón Ruiz

Reviewers
BJ Peter DeLaCruz
Kyrre Havik Eriksen
Ankit Garg

Commissioning Editor
Veena Pagare

Acquisition Editor
Reshma Raman

Content Development Editor
Rashmi Suvarna

Technical Editor
Parag Topre

Copy Editor
Shruti Iyer

Project Coordinator
Judie Jose

Proofreader
Safis Editing

Indexer
Monica Ajmera Mehta

Graphics
Disha Haria
Abhinash Sahu

Production Coordinator
Conidon Miranda

Cover Work
Conidon Miranda

About the Author

Antonio Pachón Ruiz is a software engineer with a master's degree in mobile technologies. He has more than five years of experience working as an Android developer and has developed a large number of apps.

Antonio was born in southern Spain and currently lives in London working as an Android contractor; he works part time developing for different companies, such as TomTom, MasterCard, and the UK giant, British Telecom. His experience extends from small start-ups to big telecom companies. Video streaming apps, newsreader apps, Voice over IP, voice authentication, e-commerce, online payments, navigation, and games are some of the technologies Antonio has worked on.

He is also the director of SuitApps, a venture outsourcing apps remotely for other companies, where he leads and coaches a team of developers and UI/UX designers.

Apart from the app development industry, Antonio has experience in the online teaching industry as an instructor of a course about getting started with Android with more than 8,000 students and a five-star rating.

I would like to extend great thanks to Sarah Lyon for her patience, help, and support during the writing sessions, making the book more readable and providing the images and assets needed.

I would also like to thank everyone from the SuitApps team and my amazing friends, including Sarah Lyon, a UI/UX designer; Jose Luis Neira, an Android developer; Alex Nabrozidis, an expert in Android-automated testing; and Unathi Chonco, an iOS developer.

Finally, I would like to thank the Packt Publishing team, especially Rashmi Suvarna and Reshma Raman.

About the Reviewers

BJ Peter DeLaCruz graduated with a master's degree in computer science from the University of Hawaii at Manoa. He started his career as a software developer at Referentia Systems, Inc. in Honolulu, Hawaii, where he helped develop a network performance management software called LiveAction. After working at Referentia, he was hired as a Java web developer by the University of Hawaii where he upgraded Laulima, a learning management system based on Sakai that the university uses for traditional face-to-face, online, and hybrid classes. He is currently employed by Hawaii Information Consortium (https://portal.ehawaii.gov/), where he develops web applications for the State of Hawaii.

BJ is a successful Android developer with seven Android apps published on Google Play. He is certified by Oracle in Java 8 programming and holds three certifications from CompTIA: Security+, Cloud+, and Storage+ Powered by SNIA.

BJ has also reviewed *Gradle in Action*, *Manning Publications* and *Learning Android Application Testing*, *Packt Publishing*.

During his free time, he teaches himself Japanese, reads books on the Japanese culture, and watches anime. BJ also enjoys shooting videos and uploading them to YouTube.

You can learn more about him by visiting his website, www.bjpeter.com, or contact him directly via e-mail at bj.peter.delacruz@gmail.com.

I would like to thank God, Paushali Desai, and Judie Jose for giving me the opportunity to review this book.

Kyrre Havik Eriksen is an independent and curious person with a master's degree in informatics from University of Oslo, Norway. He works full time as a Java developer, but in his spare time he studies Android, game development with Löve 2D and libGDX, and Ruby. He is currently working on getting his pet project, Tag Story (`http://tagstory.no/`), up and running. Tag Story is an interactive and social mobile game, designed to let you experience the psychical environment in a new and exciting way.

Ankit Garg works as a mobile engineer for AOL. He works in product research and development team. He has around 5 years of experience in developing mobile applications and is really passionate about making user-friendly mobile apps.

www.PacktPub.com

Support files, eBooks, discount offers, and more

For support files and downloads related to your book, please visit www.PacktPub.com.

Did you know that Packt offers eBook versions of every book published, with PDF and ePub files available? You can upgrade to the eBook version at www.PacktPub.com and as a print book customer, you are entitled to a discount on the eBook copy. Get in touch with us at service@packtpub.com for more details.

At www.PacktPub.com, you can also read a collection of free technical articles, sign up for a range of free newsletters and receive exclusive discounts and offers on Packt books and eBooks.

https://www2.packtpub.com/books/subscription/packtlib

Do you need instant solutions to your IT questions? PacktLib is Packt's online digital book library. Here, you can search, access, and read Packt's entire library of books.

Why subscribe?

- Fully searchable across every book published by Packt
- Copy and paste, print, and bookmark content
- On demand and accessible via a web browser

Free access for Packt account holders

If you have an account with Packt at www.PacktPub.com, you can use this to access PacktLib today and view 9 entirely free books. Simply use your login credentials for immediate access.

Table of Contents

Preface

This book is a practical guide to learning the development of advanced Android apps. This book helps master the core concepts of Android and quickly apply the knowledge in real-life projects. Throughout the book, an app is created, evolved in every chapter, so that the reader can easily follow and absorb the concepts.

The book is divided into twelve chapters. The first three chapters are focused on the design of the app, explaining the basic concepts of design and the programming patterns used in Android. The next few chapters aim to improve the application, accessing the server side to download the information to be shown in the app. Once the app is functionally complete, it is improved using Material Design components and other third-party libraries.

Before finishing, extra services are added to the app, such as location services, analytics, crash reports, and monetization. Finally, the app is exported, explaining the different build types and certificates, and uploaded to Play Store, ready to be distributed.

What this book covers

Chapter 1, *Getting Started*, explains the basics of Android 6 Marshmallow and important concepts of Material Design. We will set up the tools needed to start developing and, optionally, we will install an ultrafast emulator that is quicker than the Android default one, which will help us test our app along the book.

Chapter 2, *Designing our App*, introduces the first step of creating an app — designing the navigation — and the different navigation patterns. We will apply the Tabs pattern with sliding screens, explaining and using Fragments, which is a key component in the Android app development.

Chapter 3, Creating and Accessing Content from the Cloud, covers all that is necessary to display information from the Internet in our app. This information can be on an external server or API. We will create our own server using Parse, and we will access it with advanced network requests using Volley and OKHttp, processing the information and converting it into usable objects using Gson.

Chapter 4, Concurrency and Software Design Patterns, talks about concurrency in Android and the different mechanisms to handle it, such as AsyncTask, Services, Loaders, and more. The second part of this chapter talks about the most common programming patterns used in Android.

Chapter 5, Lists and Grids, discusses lists and grids, starting with ListViews. It explains how this component evolved in RecyclerView, and as an example, it shows how to create a list with different types of elements on it.

Chapter 6, CardView and Material Design, focuses on improving the app from a user interface perspective and introduces Material Design, explaining and implementing features such as CardView, Toolbar, and CoordinatorLayout.

Chapter 7, Image Handling and Memory Management, mostly talks about displaying images in our app that are downloaded from the Internet using different mechanisms such as Volley or Picasso. It also covers different types of images, such as Vector Drawable and Nine patch. Finally, it talks about memory management and preventing, detecting, and locating memory leaks.

Chapter 8, Databases and Loaders, essentially explains how databases work in Android, what content providers are, and how to get the database to communicate directly with the views using CursorLoaders.

Chapter 9, Push Notifications and Analytics, talks about how to implement push notification using Google Cloud Messaging and Parse. The second part of the chapter talks about analytics, which is critical to understand how users behave with our app, to capture error reports, and to keep our app free of bugs.

Chapter 10, Location Services, introduces MapView by implementing an example in the app from the initial setup in the developer console to the final map view in the app showing locations markers.

Chapter 11, Debugging and Testing on Android, talks mostly about testing. It covers unit test, integration, and user interface tests. It also discusses using different tools and best practices on the market to develop a maintainable app through automated tests.

Chapter 12, Monetization, the Build Process, and Release, shows how to monetize the app and explains the key concepts of advertisement monetization. It shows how to export an app with different build types and, finally, how to upload and market this app in Google Play Store.

What you need for this book

Your system must have following software to execute the code mentioned in this book:

- Android Studio 1.0 or later versions
- Java 1.7 or later versions
- Android 4.0 or later versions

Who this book is for

If you are a Java or project developer with some experience in Gradle and want to become an expert, then this book is for you. Basic knowledge of Gradle is essential.

Conventions

In this book, you will find a number of text styles that distinguish between different kinds of information. Here are some examples of these styles and an explanation of their meaning.

Code words in text, database table names, folder names, filenames, file extensions, pathnames and dummy URLs are shown as follows: "We can include other contexts through the use of the `include` directive."

A block of code is set as follows:

```
<uses-permission android:name="android.permission.INTERNET" /> <uses-
permission android:name="android.permission.ACCESS_NETWORK_STATE"
/> <uses-permission android:name="android.permission.WRITE_EXTERNAL_
STORAGE" />
```

When we wish to draw your attention to a particular part of a code block, the relevant lines or items are set in bold:

```
<uses-permission android:name="android.permission.INTERNET" /> <uses-
permission android:name="android.permission.ACCESS_NETWORK_STATE"
/> <uses-permission android:name="android.permission.WRITE_EXTERNAL_
STORAGE" />
```

New terms and **important words** are shown in bold. Words that you see on the screen, for example, in menus or dialog boxes, appear in the text like this: "Clicking the **Next** button moves you to the next screen."

Warnings or important notes appear in a box like this.

 Tips and tricks appear like this.

Reader feedback

Feedback from our readers is always welcome. Let us know what you think about this book—what you liked or disliked. Reader feedback is important for us as it helps us develop titles that you will really get the most out of.

To send us general feedback, simply e-mail feedback@packtpub.com, and mention the book's title in the subject of your message.

If there is a topic that you have expertise in and you are interested in either writing or contributing to a book, see our author guide at www.packtpub.com/authors.

Customer support

Now that you are the proud owner of a Packt book, we have a number of things to help you to get the most from your purchase.

Downloading the example code

You can download the example code files from your account at http://www.packtpub.com for all the Packt Publishing books you have purchased. If you purchased this book elsewhere, you can visit http://www.packtpub.com/support and register to have the files e-mailed directly to you.

Downloading the color images of this book

We also provide you with a PDF file that has color images of the screenshots/diagrams used in this book. The color images will help you better understand the changes in the output. You can download this file from http://www.packtpub.com/sites/default/files/downloads/4221OS_ColorImages.pdf.

Errata

Although we have taken every care to ensure the accuracy of our content, mistakes do happen. If you find a mistake in one of our books—maybe a mistake in the text or the code—we would be grateful if you could report this to us. By doing so, you can save other readers from frustration and help us improve subsequent versions of this book. If you find any errata, please report them by visiting http://www.packtpub.com/submit-errata, selecting your book, clicking on the **Errata Submission Form** link, and entering the details of your errata. Once your errata are verified, your submission will be accepted and the errata will be uploaded to our website or added to any list of existing errata under the Errata section of that title.

To view the previously submitted errata, go to https://www.packtpub.com/books/content/support and enter the name of the book in the search field. The required information will appear under the **Errata** section.

Piracy

Piracy of copyrighted material on the Internet is an ongoing problem across all media. At Packt, we take the protection of our copyright and licenses very seriously. If you come across any illegal copies of our works in any form on the Internet, please provide us with the location address or website name immediately so that we can pursue a remedy.

Please contact us at copyright@packtpub.com with a link to the suspected pirated material.

We appreciate your help in protecting our authors and our ability to bring you valuable content.

Questions

If you have a problem with any aspect of this book, you can contact us at questions@packtpub.com, and we will do our best to address the problem.

1
Getting Started

We will start the book with an overview of Material Design and Android 6 Marshmallow. The new Material Design concept from Google has been a revolution in the way apps look and feel.

During the course of the book, we will build an app called `MasteringAndroidApp`. In this chapter, we will explain what the app is about. In this app, we will put into practice all the concepts and theory explained in every chapter. At the end of the book, we should have a rich app, full of features, which can be easily modified to create your own version and uploaded to the Google Play Store.

We will ensure that we have all the necessary tools, downloading the latest version of Android and introducing **Genymotion**, the quickest emulator for Android, strongly recommended for this book.

- Material Design
- Key points for Android 6 Marshmallow
- Overview of the App
- Getting the tools ready
    - Android Studio
    - SDK Manager
- Genymotion

Introducing Material Design

As mentioned earlier, Material Design was a revolution in the way apps look and feel. You have probably heard of this concept before, but what is it exactly?

Material Design is a new visual language created by Google, used on all the platforms, websites, and mobile devices that are based on materials, meaningful transitions, animations, and responsive interactions.

The material is a metaphor of an element that can be seen on the surface; it consists of layers that can have different heights and widths, but their thickness is always one unit, as with sheets of paper. We can place materials above each other, which introduces a depth element to the view, a Z coordinate. In the same way, we can have a sheet of paper on top of another, casting shadows and defining a visual priority.

The content is displayed on the materials but they don't add thickness to it. The content can be displayed in any shape and color; it can be a plain background color, a text, a video, and many other things. It is limited within the bounds of the material.

The material can expand and the content can expand with it, but the content can never expand more than the material. We can't have two materials at the same Z position. One of them always has to be below or on top of the other. If we interact with the materials, we always interact at the top layer level. For instance, a touch event will be performed in the top layer and won't go through to the layers below. You can change the size and shape of the materials and the two materials can be merged into one, but they can't bend or fold.

This is an example of an app using the Material Design style; we can see cards with shadows, different content, and an app bar with a navigation drawer. All these components will be explained in the course of this book, and we will aim to build an app using the same style.

Material design also came with important UI elements, such as `RecyclerView`. This is a view that will replace `ListView`, which came earlier in Android, to create any kind of a scrollable list of elements. We'll work with these components in *Chapter 5*, *Lists and Grids*, starting with the basic version of `ListView`, evolving it to understand how `RecyclerView` was born, and finishing with an example of it.

The `CardView` was another major UI element introduced. We can see one in the previous image; it's a component with a background and shadows that can be customized to fit all the content that we want. We will work with it in *Chapter 6*, *CardView and Material Design*, where we'll also introduce the next component — design support library.

Design support library is a *must have* library that includes animations, **FAB (Floating Action Button)**, and the navigation drawer. You've probably already seen the sliding menu that comes from the left in other apps. Design support library offers support for these components in previous Android versions, allowing us to use Material Design features in older versions.

All of the above are features from a UI and programming perspective, but Material design also introduced different features for our phone, such as a new notification management system with different priority levels. For instance, we can say which notifications are important and establish a time frame when we don't want to be disturbed.

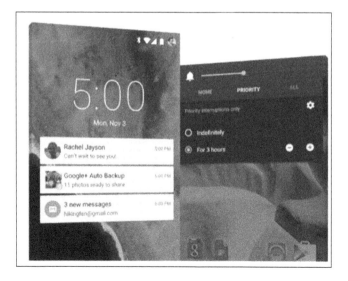

Another thing that we can't miss is the battery consumption improvement in this version, which can save up to 90 minutes of battery compared to previous Android versions, and it is due to a new Android runtime called ART. To explain it in a nontechnical way, it translates the app to a language that can be understood by Android faster when the app is installed. The previous runtime, **Dalvik**, had to do this translation while executing our app rather than just once at the installation. This helps the app consume less battery and run faster.

Introducing Android 6 Marshmallow

One of the main changes in this version has to do with the permissions for apps. Before Android M, we were used to accepting the permissions of an app when we were about to download it; the play store showed us a list of permissions that an app has, and we needed to accept them in order to download and install it.

Runtime permissions

This has changed with the introduction of runtime permissions. The idea here is to accept the permission only when you need it. For instance, WhatsApp might not need access to your microphone until your make a call or leave a voice message.

This is something we need to take into account when we develop an app; it is a change for the developer who now needs to control what is to be done if the user doesn't accept the permission. Previously, we didn't have to do any controlling because it was an all-or-none choice at installation time; now, we have to consider the decision of the user at runtime.

Downloading the example code

You can download the example code files from your account at http://www.packtpub.com for all the Packt Publishing books you have purchased. If you purchased this book elsewhere, you can visit http://www.packtpub.com/support and register to have the files e-mailed directly to you.

Power-saving optimizations

There is another improvement regarding the battery life of our phones since Lollipop; this time, Google has introduced two new states: **doze mode** and **app standby**.

Doze mode improves the sleep efficiency of idle devices. If we turn off the screen and are not using the phone, we enter the idle state. Previously, applications could do network operations and continue working in the background; now, with the introduction of doze mode, the system periodically allows our apps to work in the background and perform other pending operations for a brief period of time. Again, this brings in some consideration while developing; for instance, in this mode, our apps can't access the network.

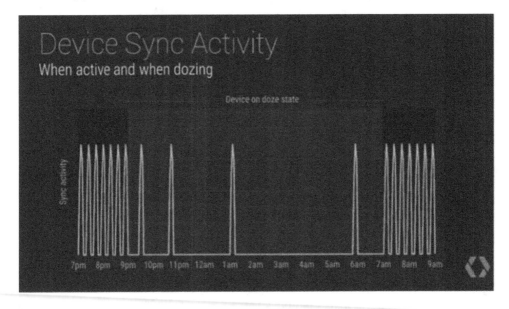

App standby is an induced idle mode for an app that has not been used for a while and doesn't have any processes running in the background. It is used for an app if it does not show any notifications and if the user has not explicitly asked it to be exempt from optimization. This idle mode prevents the app from accessing the network and executing pending jobs. When the power cable is connected, all apps in a standby state are released, and the idle restrictions are removed.

Text selection

In the previous versions, when a user selected text, a set of actions appeared on the action bar, such as copy, cut, and paste. With this version, we can show these actions and more, in a floating bar that will be presented above the selection:

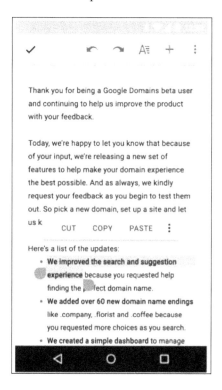

Fingerprint authentication

In this version of Android, we can authenticate the use of our fingerprint. The authentication can be at a device level to unlock the phone, not just to unlock a specific app; so, we can authenticate users in our app based on how recently they unlocked their device.

We have a new object available, `FingerprintManager`, which will be in charge of the authentication and allow us to show a dialog requesting the fingerprint. We would need a device with a fingerprint sensor in order to use this feature.

Direct share

Direct share is a new addition to simplify the content sharing process. Previously, if we were in the gallery and wanted to share a picture to a contact in WhatsApp, we had to click on **Share**, find WhatsApp in the list of apps, and then find a contact inside WhatsApp to share this content. This process will be simplified, showing a list of contacts with whom you can share the information directly:

These are the main new features that have been released with Android 6 Marshmallow; the complete list can be seen at http://developer.android.com/preview/index.html.

Creating MasteringAndroidApp

Now that we've seen the main features of the latest Android version, we can introduce the app that we are going to develop during the book. This app will include most of these features, but we will also spend time in the components widely used in previous Android versions.

To master Android, we should be prepared to understand legacy code; for instance, we might have to work on an app that still uses `ListView` instead of `RecyclerView`, which is new. We will not always create apps from scratch with the latest components, especially if we are professional Android developers. Also, looking at previous components will help us understand the natural evolution of these components to have a better idea of how they are now.

We will start creating this app totally from scratch, starting with the initial design, having a look at the most used design and navigation patterns in Android, such as tabs at the top, a sliding menu on the left side, and so on.

The app that we will develop, `MasteringAndroidApp`, is one with server-side interaction. This app will show information that is stored in the cloud, and we will create the cloud component, making our app communicate with it. The topic we have chosen for the app is a job listing board, where we will create job offers on the server side, and the users of the app can read these offers and receive notifications.

You can easily customize the topic; this will be an example where you can change the information and create your own app with the same structure. In fact, it's better if you think of your own idea because we will discuss how to publish the app in Play Store and how to monetize it; we will add adverts, which will generate revenue when the users click on it. So, if you apply what you learn using your idea, by the time you finish the book, you will have an app ready to be distributed.

We will develop the app explaining the programming patterns that are most used in Android as well as concurrency techniques and different methods to connect to rest APIs or servers.

We'll not only be focusing on the backend, but also on the UI; by displaying the information in an efficient way, using lists and grids, downloading images from the Internet, and customizing fonts and views with the latest material design features.

We will learn the mechanism for debugging our apps, managing logs, and consider the memory usage while learning how to identify and prevent memory leaks.

Our app will have an offline mode based on a database, where we will store the content from the cloud. So, if the mobile loses connection, we can still show the information available when we were last online.

To complete our app, we will add extra features such as push notifications, crash reports, and analytics.

To finish, we will see how the Android build system works, exporting our app in different versions as well as obfuscating the code to protect it and prevent decompiling.

We have compressed a huge amount of information that will help you to master Android by the end of the book; however, before starting with our app, let's get the tools ready.

Getting the tools ready

The tools that we will need during the book are the latest version of Android Studio, an Android SDK updated to Android M or later. It is also recommended that you have **Genymotion**, an emulator to test the app.

> First, we need to download and install Android Studio, the official tool to develop in Android. It can be downloaded from `http://developer.android.com/sdk/index.html`.

At the top of the website, you will have a link to download it depending on your OS version.

Once it's installed, we need to download an Android M SDK, which will provide all the classes and resources necessary to develop an app for a specific Android version. This is done through SDK Manager, a tool included inside Android Studio.

We can click on **Tools** | **Android** | **SDK Manager** or find a shortcut in the uppermost bar of Android Studio.

Once we open SDK manager, we will see a list of the available SDK platforms and SDK tools. We need to ensure that the latest version available is installed.

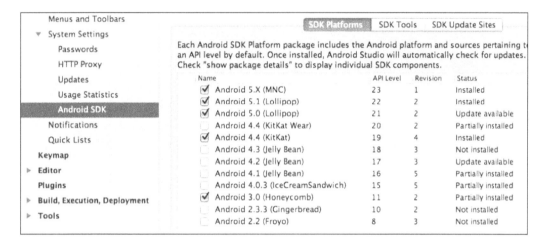

With this, we have all that we need to develop our app. In order to test it, it would be ideal to have Genymotion, which is an Android emulator that will help us test our app on different devices.

The reason we use this emulator instead of the Android default one is primarily the speed. Deploying an app in Genymotion is even quicker than using a physical device. Apart from this, we benefit from other features, such as resizable windows, copying and pasting from our computer, and other smaller details that are time consuming with the default emulator. It can be downloaded from `https://www.genymotion.com`.

All we need to do is install it, and once opened, we can add emulators with the same features included with existing devices.

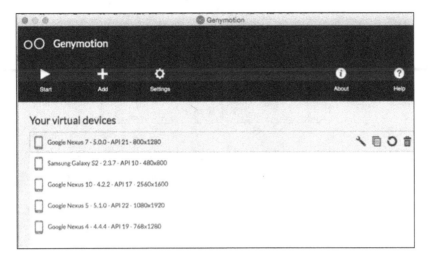

Summary

In this chapter, we went through the important changes in the latest versions of Android, highlighting Android Marshmallow and Material Design.

We explained what we will do in the app that we'll be building through the course of this book and the tools that we'll need to create it.

In the next chapter, we will look at the existing design patterns in Android and start designing our app.

2
Designing our App

In this chapter, we will think of an idea for an app and transform that idea into a real app, create a basic structure to be displayed on the screen, and choose an appropriate navigation pattern to move between them.

After taking a look at the most commonly used navigation pattern, we will proceed with implementing the tabs pattern composed by fragment and `ViewPager`.

During this, we will do a review of our knowledge of fragments to be able to explain the advanced concepts. We will also discuss the importance of `FragmentManager` and the fragments back-stack.

To finish, we will add some good-looking animations to our screen transitions. Therefore, we will cover the following topics in this chapter:

- Selecting an app navigation pattern
- Mastering fragments
- Implementing tabs and ViewPager
- Animated transitions between screens

Selecting an app-navigation pattern

Let's imagine that one day you wake up feeling inspired; you have an idea for an app that you believe can become more popular than WhatsApp. Without losing time, you would want to turn this app idea into reality! This is why it's important for you to learn how to design an app and choose the most appropriate navigation pattern. Not to sound uninspiring, but you'll find that 99 percent of your ideas will already be on Google Play Store. It's simply a fact that there are hundreds of thousands of apps available, and the number is always increasing! So, you can either decide to improve upon the already existing ones or keep brainstorming until you have something original.

In order to make the app a reality, the first step is to visualize the app in your mind; for this, we need to identify the basic components. We need to simplify the idea on screen, and we need to move between screens.

Bear in mind that you are creating this app for Android users. These users are used to using navigation patterns such as the sliding panel, which is used in apps such as Gmail, Facebook, and Spotify.

We will take a look at three different and commonly used navigation patterns that guarantee that the user won't get lost in our app and will understand the app structure instantly.

Basic structure

In order to draw our screens (note that I am not referring to activities or fragments yet; by screen I mean what the user can literally see on screen at any point during the execution of our app), we need to identify the key points of our idea. We need to establish the use cases, speaking in software development terms.

Let's start by giving shape to the app that we will build during the course of this book: **MasteringAndroidApp**. It's difficult to visualize all the details in your mind at first, so we will start by identifying the components that we know we need for sure and later fill in the gaps if there are any.

We know from the previous chapter that we have a presentation screen, which shows the logo of the app for a few seconds while downloading data from the Internet if needed.

In this app, we will also have a screen with a list of the information coming from the Internet, with individual items that the user can click on to get more detailed information.

As the main option, we will show a contact screen with `MapView` showing my location and contact data.

To finish, we need a **Preferences** or **Settings** screen, where we can turn on and off the notifications and deactivate ads or purchase extras.

Now, we are ready to create a mock-up. Have a look at the following image:

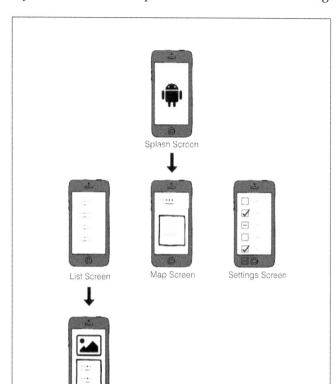

At the top, we have the entry point of our application, which is the splash screen. The navigation here is straightforward; we can navigate to the next screen in a straight line, and there are no buttons or any other possible flow.

On the next level, we have a screen with the list of items (which is a screen with contact information), a map view, and a settings screen. These three screens are at the same level in our app, so they have the same importance.

Finally, we have a third level of navigation, which is the detailed view of an item of the list.

The only way we can open this screen is by clicking on an element of the list; so, the entry point of this screen is the list screen.

Now that we have a basic structure and flow created, we will look through the different extensively used navigation patterns in order to decide which one would work best for our app.

 For more information on the app structure and similar information on material design, refer to the following links:

https://developer.android.com/design/patterns/app-structure.html

http://www.google.com/design/spec/patterns/app-structure.html#

The dashboard pattern

The dashboard pattern is one of the first patterns used in Android. It consists of a set of elements displayed on the main screen as a matrix of icons. In the following image, we can see one of the first versions of the Facebook app on the left-hand side, and to the right, a customization of the pattern from Motor Trend:

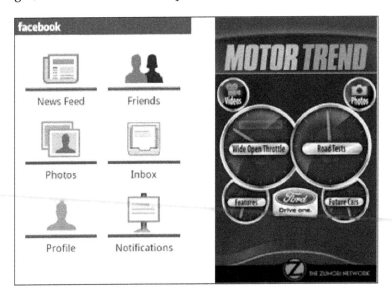

This view is great for apps that aim to display a very limited number of options clearly; there are no more than two elements per row with a number of rows that fits on the screen.

These icons clearly display symbols of the main functionality with all the options at the same level. It's an ideal pattern for apps that have a large target audience; it's straightforward and self explanatory, so anyone can navigate it.

Even though this design seems old, given that it was extensively used in the first versions of Android and is used less nowadays, its usage depends on your needs, so don't let this put you off. The Motor Trends app shown in the preceding image had a very original implementation of this pattern.

If the elements don't fit on the screen and we need to scroll in order to discover them, we need to reconsider the pattern. The same thing applies when we have too few elements; there are better options for these cases. In our particular example, we have three main elements, so we will not use this pattern.

The sliding panel

This pattern is well known thanks to apps such as Gmail and Facebook. It presents a layout at the top level of the UI; screens come out from the left or right when we perform a swipe gesture or click on the top left or right button, which usually is an icon displayed with three horizontal lines—also know as the Hamburger icon.

This pattern is perfect if we have a large number of options at the same level in our app, and it can be combined with other patterns, such as **the tabs pattern**.

The implementation of this panel can be done with the DrawerLayout class, which is composed of two child views: a FrameLayout with the content and the navigation drawer, which can be ListView or any other custom layout containing the options.

For this, execute the following code:

```
<android.support.v4.widget.DrawerLayout xmlns:android="http://schemas.
android.com/apk/res/android"
    android:id="@+id/drawer_layout"
    android:layout_width="match_parent"
    android:layout_height="match_parent" >

    <FrameLayout
      android:id="@+id/frame_container"
      android:layout_width="match_parent"
      android:layout_height="match_parent" />

    <ListView
      android:id="@+id/drawer_list"
      android:layout_width="240dp"
      android:background="#fff"
      android:layout_height="match_parent"
      android:layout_gravity="start" />

</android.support.v4.widget.DrawerLayout>
```

Once we select an element in this side panel, a child appears in the middle of the screen; this child can help you navigate to a subchild but never to an element of the main menu. The child and sub child navigation can be managed with the back button or the up navigation in the action bar.

We can close the panel by clicking on an item and know whether the panel is closed or open by setting a drawer listener, `ActionBarDrawerToggle`, which contains the `onDrawerClosed(View drawerView)` and `onDrawerOpened(View drawerView)` methods.

Ensure that you use `ActionBarDrawerToggle` from `android.support.v7.app`; the one included in v4 is deprecated.

Another big advantage of this pattern is that it allows group navigation via a main item on the menu that can be expanded into subitems. As you can see in the following example, Item 4 has three options inside it in a drop-down menu:

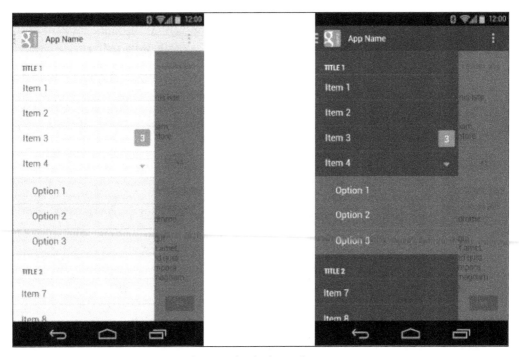

An example of a drawer layout

This would not be suitable for our app as we don't have enough options to make the most of this pattern. Also, as this pattern can be combined with the tabs pattern, it makes more sense from an educational perspective to develop our example with this pattern.

Tabs

The tabs pattern is a pattern that you have probably seen and used before.

It shows a fixed menu with components at the same level. Note that when we have tabs, the menu is always visible, which doesn't happen in the sliding and dashboard patterns. This looks very similar to a web interface and is very user friendly considering that the user probably already knows this pattern.

The following pattern has two variants: fixed and sliding tabs. If we only have a small number of menu items that can fit on the screen, the first variant will be the most suitable as it shows the users all the items at once.

Sliding tabs are usually used when all the items don't fit on the screen or when they do fit but we know that more items will be added and won't fit in the future.

The implementation of the two variants is slightly different, so we need to consider future changes when deciding the variant. Here, we can see an implementation of a sliding variant:

 Remember that for platform consistency, we must place the tabs at the top of the screen; otherwise, people will think that you are an iOS developer!

Here are some features and formatting specifications from the material design guidelines for you to follow:

- Present tabs as a single row. Wrap tab labels to a second line if needed and then truncate.
- Do not include a set of tabbed content within a tab.
- Highlight the tab corresponding to the visible content.
- Group tabs together hierarchically. Connect a group of tabs with its content.
- Keep tabs adjacent to their content. It helps maintain the relationship between the two with less ambiguity.

In the following image, we can see an example of scrolling/sliding tabs with a submenu:

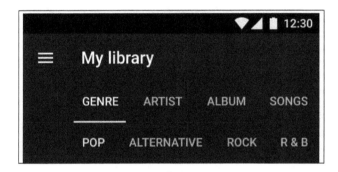

 The graphic specifications while designing tabs along with more information about label specs can be found at http://www.google.com/design/spec/components/tabs.html#.

Now that we know the basics of app navigation, we can explore the components that we need to implement these patterns. The main components, as you know, are activities and fragments. We are going to implement an example of sliding tabs with three fragments.

Fragments

In this section, we are going to review briefly the key concepts of fragments to explain advanced features and components, such as Fragment Manager and the fragments back stack.

In our example, we will create an activity called `MainActivity` and four fragments: `ListFragment`, `ContactFragment`, `SettingsFragment`, and `DetailsFragment`. For this, you can create a `fragments` package and double-click on the package to go to **New | Fragment | Blank Fragment**. Take a look at the following dialog box:

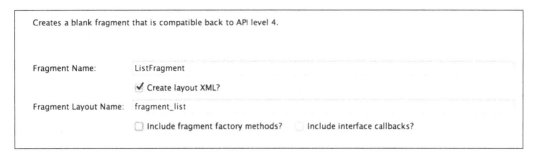

For now, you can create them without the fragment factory methods and the interface callbacks. We will cover these later in the chapter.

Our project so far should look like this in the **Project** view:

Understanding the importance of fragments

A fragment represents a behavior or a portion of the user interface in an activity. You can combine multiple fragments in a single activity to build a multipane UI and reuse a fragment in multiple activities. You can think of a fragment as a modular section of an activity that has its own lifecycle and receives its own input events, which you can add or remove while the activity is running (sort of like a *subactivity* that you can reuse in different activities).

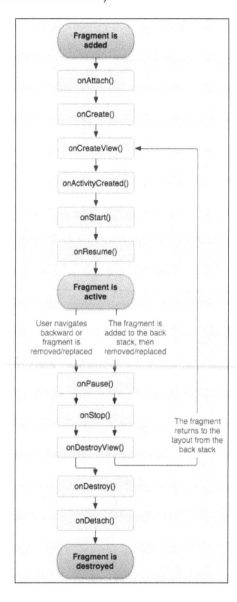

The fragment lifecycle is slightly different from the activity lifecycle. The first difference we notice is the use of the `OnAttach()` and `OnDetach()` methods, which connect the fragment to the activity.

Using `onCreate()`, we can create the view in `OnCreateView()`; after this we can call `getView()` in our fragment, and it won't be null.

The `onActivityCreated()` method tells the fragment that its activity has been completed on its own `Activity.onCreate()`.

There are two ways to display a fragment:

The first way is to have the fragment in our layout XML. This will create our fragment when the view containing it is inflated. Execute the following code:

```
<LinearLayout xmlns:android="http://schemas.android.com/apk/res/
android"
    android:orientation="horizontal"
    android:layout_width="fill_parent"
    android:layout_height="fill_parent">

    <fragment android:name="com.example.android.MyFragment"
            android:id="@+id/headlines_fragment"
android:layout_width="match_parent"
            android:layout_height="match_parent" />
</LinearLayout>
```

The second way is to create our fragment programmatically and tell Fragment Manager to display it in a container. For this, you can use the following code:

```
<LinearLayout xmlns:android="http://schemas.android.com/apk/res/
android"
    android:orientation="horizontal"
    android:layout_width="fill_parent"
    android:layout_height="fill_parent">

    <Framelayout android:id="@+id/fragment_container"
android:layout_width="match_parent"
            android:layout_height="match_parent" />

</LinearLayout>
```

After this, inflate a `FrameLayout` container where the fragment will be inserted using the following lines of code:

```
Myfragment fragment = MyFragment.newInstance();
getSupportFragmentManager().beginTransaction()
                    .add(R.id.fragment_container, fragment).commit();
```

To finish with the key concepts, it is important to explain why Android examples create the fragments using the `MyFragment.newInstance(params)` factory method instead of using the default new `MyFragment(params)` constructor. Take a look at the following code:

```
public class MyFragment extends Fragment {

  // Static factory method that returns a new fragment
  // receiving a    parameter and initializing the fragment's arguments

    public static MyFragment newInstance(int param) {
        MyFragment fragment = new MyFragment();
        Bundle args = new Bundle();
        args.putInt("param", param);
        fragment.setArguments(args);
        return fragment;
    }
}
```

The reason behind this pattern is that Android only recreates Fragments using the default constructor; therefore, if we have a constructor with parameters, it will be ignored, and the parameters will be lost.

Note that we send the parameters in a bundle as arguments, allowing the fragment to retrieve the parameter if it has to be recreated (due to a device orientation change, we use the back navigation).

The Fragment Manager

The Fragment Manager is an interface used to interact with the fragments inside an activity. This means that any operation, such as adding, replacing, removing, or finding a fragment, has to be done through it.

To obtain Fragment Manager, our `Activity` needs to extend from `FragmentActivity`, which will allows us to call `getFragmentManager()` or `getSupportFragmentManager()` preferably that maintain backwards compatibility using the Fragment Manager included in `Android.support.v4`.

If we want to use nested fragments, we can manage them with
`getChildFragmentManager()`. You cannot inflate a layout into a fragment when this
layout includes `<fragment>`. Nested fragments are only supported when added to a
fragment dynamically.

Now, we will discuss some scenarios that we will face sooner or later while working
with fragments. Imagine that we have an activity with two fragments, A and B.

A typical scenario is that we are in a fragment and we want to execute a method from
the activity. In this case, we have two options; one is to implement a `public` method
in `MyActivity`, for instance `doSomething()`, so that we can cast `getActivity` to our
activity and call the `((MyActivity)getActivity).doSomething();` method.

The second way is to make our activity implement an interface defined in our
fragment, and make the instance of the activity a listener of this interface in our
fragment during the `onAttach(Activity)` method. We will explain this software
pattern in *Chapter 4, Concurrency and Software Design Patterns*. For the other way
around, to get an Activity to communicate with a fragment (if we don't have
fragment A instantiated in a variable in our activity), we can find the fragment in the
manager. A fragment can be found using the ID of the container or a tag that we will
take a look at in the following section:

```
FragmentManager fm = getSupportFragmentManger();
FragmentA fragmentA = fm.findFragmentById(R.id.fragment_container);
fragmentA.doSomething(params);
```

The final scenario would be in fragment A and speaking to B; for this, we just need
to retrieve the manager from the activity and find the fragment. Run the following
code:

```
FragmentManager fm = getActivity().getSupportFragmentManger();
FragmentA fragmentA = fm.findFragmentById(R.id.fragment_container);
fragmentA.doSomething(params);
```

Fragments stack

We have been speaking about finding a fragment in fragment manager and this is
possible thanks to the Fragment Manager stack of fragments where we can add or
remove fragments during transactions.

When we want to display a fragment dynamically, we can decide whether we want
to add the fragment to the stack or not. Having the fragment on the stack allows us
to navigate back to the previous fragment.

This is important for our example; if the user is on the first tab and clicks on an item on the list, we want him/her to see the details screen, DetailsFragment. Now, if the user is on DetailsFragment and clicks on the back button, we don't want him/her to leave the App; we want the app to navigate back to the fragment stack. This is why when we add DetailsFragment, we have to include the addToBackStack(String tag) option. The tag can either be null, or it can be a String type that will allow us to find this new fragment by the tag. It will look similar to the following:

```
FragmentTransaction ft = getFragmentManager().beginTransaction();
ft.replace(R.id.simple_fragment, newFragment);
ft.addToBackStack(null);
ft.commit();
```

To clarify further, if we wanted to navigate between three fragments, *A to B to C*, and then navigate back, having a stack will allow us to go *C to B to A*. However, if we don't add the fragments to the back stack or if we add or replace them in the same container, *A to B to C*, this will leave us with only the C fragment and without the back navigation.

Now, to implement the back navigation in DetailsFragment, we have to let the activity know that when I click on back, I want to first navigate back in the fragment before quitting the app, as it does by default. This can be done by overriding onKeyDown and handling the fragment navigation if there is more than one fragment in the back stack. Run the following command:

```
@Override
public boolean onKeyDown(int keyCode, KeyEvent event) {
if (keyCode == KeyEvent.KEYCODE_BACK && getSupportFragmentManager.
getBackStackEntryCount > 1) {
getSupportFragment.popBackStack();
return true;
}
return super.onKeyDown(keyCode, event);
}
```

ViewPager

Continuing with our example, we have two ways of navigating between fragments on `MainActivity`: either by tapping on the tabs or by swiping between the fragments. To achieve this, we will use `ViewPager`, including the sliding tabs inside it, which is a very elegant solution with minimal code and includes synchronization between swipe and tabs.

`ViewPager` can be used to slide any kind of view. We could create a gallery of images with `ViewPager`; it is very common to see tutorials in the first run of some apps where you can slide the screen with instructions on how the app works, and this is achieved with `ViewPager`. To add `ViewPager` to `MainActivity`, we can simply copy and paste the following code:

```xml
<?xml version="1.0" encoding="utf-8"?>
<android.support.v4.view.ViewPager
xmlns:android="http://schemas.android.com/apk/res/android"
android:id="@+id/pager"
android:layout_width="match_parent"
android:layout_height="match_parent" />
```

At the end of the *ViewPager* section, we will see how to use different third party libraries to improve the experience with tabs and also how to create these tabs manually in case we want our custom solution.

Adapter

`ViewPager` works with an adapter; the adapter is the element in charge of creating every *page* that we swipe. In the particular case of swiping fragments, there are extensions of the `Adapter` class called `FragmentPagerAdapter` and `FragmentStatePagerAdapter` that we can use:

- `FragmentStatePagerAdapter` saves the state of the page, destroys it when it does not appear on screen, and recreates it when necessary, similar to what `ListView` does with its rows.

- `FragmentPagerAdapter` keeps all the pages in memory; therefore, it doesn't have the computing cost associated with saving and restoring the state while swiping. The number of pages we can have depends on the memory.

Depending on the number of elements, we can choose one or the other. If we were creating an app to read the news, where you could swipe between lots of news articles with images and different content, we wouldn't try to have all of them in the memory.

We have three fixed tabs, so we will choose `FragmentPagerAdapter`. We will create a package adapter and create a `MyPagerAdapter` class that will extend `FragmentPagerAdapter`. While extending it, we are asked to override the `getCount()` and `getItem(int i)` methods, which return the count of the items and return an item in a given position.

After creating a constructor and completing the methods, our class will look similar to the following code:

```java
public class MyPagerAdapter extends FragmentPagerAdapter {

    public MyPagerAdapter(FragmentManager fm) {
        super(fm);
    }

    @Override
    public Fragment getItem(int i) {
        switch (i) {
            case 0 :
                return new ListFragment();
            case 1 :
                return new ContactFragment();
            case 2 :
                return new SettingsFragment();
            default:
                return null;
        }
    }

    @Override
    public int getCount() {
        return 3;
    }
}
```

To finish, we need to set the adapter to the pager in `MainActivity`. Execute the following code:

```
public class MainActivity extends FragmentActivity {

    @Override
    protected void onCreate(Bundle savedInstanceState) {
        super.onCreate(savedInstanceState);
        setContentView(R.layout.activity_main);

        MyPagerAdapter adapter = new MyPagerAdapter(getSupportFragmentManager());
        ViewPager viewPager = (ViewPager) findViewById(R.id.pager);
        viewPager.setAdapter(adapter);

    }

}
```

Sliding tabs

At this point in our example, we are able to swipe between our fragments. Now, we will add tabs using `PagerTabStrip` or `PagerTitleStrip`.

There is a very elegant way to achieve this, which is including `PageTabStrip` in the XML tag of `ViewPager`. Execute the following code:

```
<?xml version="1.0" encoding="utf-8"?>
<android.support.v4.view.ViewPager
xmlns:android="http://schemas.android.com/apk/res/android"
android:id="@+id/pager"
android:layout_width="match_parent"
android:layout_height="wrap_content">

    <android.support.v4.view.PagerTabStrip
        android:id="@+id/pager_title_strip"
        android:layout_width="match_parent"
        android:layout_height="wrap_content"
        android:layout_gravity="top"
        android:background="#33b5e5"
        android:textColor="#fff"
        android:textSize="20dp"
        android:paddingTop="10dp"
        android:paddingBottom="10dp" />

</android.support.v4.view.ViewPager>
```

Here, `PagerTabStrip` will find the tile of the page, and for each page, it will display a tab. We need to add the `getPageTitle` method in `MyPagerAdapter`, which will return a string for every page. In our case, this would be the name of the sections: list, contacts, and settings. For this, you can use the following code:

```
@Override
public CharSequence getPageTitle(int position) {
  switch (position) {
    case 0 :
    return "LIST";
    case 1 :
    return "CONTACT";
    case 2 :
    return "SETTINGS";
    default:
    return null;
  }
}
```

Run the app, and voila! We have a fluent tab and sliding navigation supporting Android 1.6 (API 4) implemented really easily:

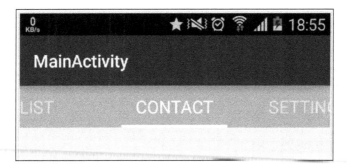

Customizing tabs

There is a long story behind tabs in Android; initially, tabs were implemented with `TabActivity` but this was deprecated in API 13 and evolved into `FragmentTabHost`.

So, I happily developed an app with `TabHost` following the Android documentation, and I realized this had to be changed. At first, I crossed my fingers hoping that the deprecation wouldn't affect my app until some users complained about crashes. Then, inevitably, I had to remove my deprecated `TabHost` and find a new way.

At first, `FragmentTabHost` seemed a good way to have fixed tabs, but it didn't allow tabs with icons on them. Upon having this problem and finding other people with the same problem in Stack Overflow at `http://stackoverflow.com/` (a website where we can ask questions and find answers on Android and other topics), I decided to find another way.

In API 11, the concept of `ActionBar.Tab` appeared, which was a class that allowed us to add tabs to the action bar. Finally, I found a way to have tabs in my app, which resulted in happy users! But this joy didn't last for long; `ActionBar.Tab` was deprecated again!!

This is something that would end up the patience of any developer; this made me create my own tabs as buttons in `LinearLayout`. Setting a click listener on the buttons and when clicking on a tab I was swiping the `ViewPager` to the right page, and the other way around, when detecting a page swipe on the `ViewPager` I was selecting the right tab. It was worth the effort because it allowed me to have all the freedom that I wanted with the tabs design, and more importantly gave me the satisfaction that it would always work (unless one day they deprecate `LinearLayout` or `Button`!).

You can always leave your own implementation as the last option. Nowadays, if you don't like the sliding tabs design, you have other alternatives from third-party libraries, such as `ViewPagerIndicator` and `PagerSlidingTabStrip`.

 To learn more about this, you can check out the following links:
`https://github.com/JakeWharton/ViewPagerIndicator`
`https://github.com/astuetz/PagerSlidingTabStrip`

Transitions

Small details such as creating our own animations from the screen transitions will polish our app and really make it look more professional.

Our example is perfect to talk about transitions as we have two types of screen transitions:

- The first one is a transition between Activities, from `SplashActivity` to `MainActivity`

- The second one (not implemented yet) is a transition between fragments, where `ListFragment` is replaced with `DetailsFragment`

For the transitions between activities, we need to call `overridePendingTransition` just before starting the new activity. The method receives two animations as parameters, and these animations can be in an XML file created by us or be chosen from the already created animations in Android. Run the following command:

```
overridePendingTransition(android.R.anim.fade_in, android.R.anim.fade_out);
```

In our example, we don't allow back navigation to `SplashActivity`; however, if we were in a transition between activities where we wanted to have the same transition when we click on back, we would have to override the back key press and set our transition there. For this, you can run the following command:

```
@Override public void onBackPressed() {
    super.onBackPressed();        overridePendingTransition(android.R.anim.fade_in,  android.R.anim.fade_out);
}
```

In the case of fragments, we need to specify the transition in the `FragmentTransaction` object. Using the object animator, we can define this in two files: `enter.xml` and `exit.xml`. Execute the following code:

```
FragmentTransaction transaction = getFragmentManager().beginTransaction();
transaction.setCustomAnimations(R.animator.enter, R.animator.exit);
transaction.replace(R.id.container, new DetailsFragment());
transaction.commit();

enter.xml

<?xml version="1.0" encoding="utf-8"?>
<set>
    <objectAnimator
        xmlns:android="http://schemas.android.com/apk/res/android"
        android:duration="1000"
        android:propertyName="y"
        android:valueFrom="2000"
        android:valueTo="0"
        android:valueType="floatType" />
</set>
```

```
exit.xml
<?xml version="1.0" encoding="utf-8"?>
<set>
    <objectAnimator
        xmlns:android="http://schemas.android.com/apk/res/android"
        android:duration="1000"
        android:propertyName="y"
        android:valueFrom="0"
        android:valueTo="-2000"
        android:valueType="floatType" />
</set>
```

For Android Lollipop and the later versions, you can set the transition directly to the Fragment. Use the following snippet:

```
Fragment f = new MyFragment();
f.setEnterTransition(new Slide(Gravity.RIGHT));
f.setExitTransition(new Slide(Gravity.LEFT));
```

Summary

At the end of this chapter, you should have an understanding of the basic navigation patterns and be able to translate the idea of an app in your mind into the real structure of an Android app. Fragments are a key concept in Android development, and we have spent enough time in this chapter mastering them with a review of Fragment Manager and the fragments back stack and by learning how to face common problems such as communication between them. We considered a working example of `ViewPager` with `PagerTabStrip` showing the tile of the pages as tabs, which you now know how to customize if needed. We have a skeleton of an app; this project can be saved at this stage and used as a template for your future developments. We are ready to continue evolving our app.

In the next chapter, we will see how to create and access the content that will populate our fragments and `ViewPager` to bring our app to life.

3
Creating and Accessing Content from the Cloud

In this chapter, we will learn how to consume content from the Web using our application; this content could be a list of items inside an XML or JSON file (something that we wish to display), retrieved from the Internet. For instance, if we were building an app that shows the current weather conditions, we would need to contact an external API to retrieve all the information needed.

We will create our own cloud database in Parse, a service that allows us to do this really quickly without the hassle of creating and maintaining our own servers. Apart from this, we will populate the database with information to be displayed in `MasteringAndroidApp`.

We will also cover best practices regarding network requests with Google Volley, using the ultrafast HTTP library, OkHttp, and parsing the requested objects efficiently with Gson. We will cover the following topics in this chapter:

- Creating your own cloud database
- Consuming content from Parse
- Google Volley and OkHttp
- Parsing objects with Gson

Creating your own cloud database

At this stage of the project, we have to start modeling our own version of `MasteringAndroidApp`. Feel free to develop your own ideas and use the database for your own data. Follow this example as a guide; you don't necessarily have to copy all the lines of code exactly as I write them. In fact, if you develop your own example at the end of this book, you will have something that you can use. For instance, you can create an app for your own personal use, such as a task reminder, travel diary, personal photo gallery — or anything else that is suitable for storage in the cloud.

You could also try to monetize this app; in this case, you should try to develop something interesting for users. For instance, it can be a news feed reader or recipes reader for food; it can be any app where you can submit content to the cloud and notify users that new content is available.

During this process, we will explain the importance of the `Application` class, which is used to set up Parse in our project.

Parse

Parse is free if you have less than 30 requests per second. I imagine that if you have enough users requesting information from your app 30 times per second, which is 1,800 per minute, you can surely afford to upgrade to a paid account or even build your own server! This service is a very easy and reliable way to have the server side covered for your app. It also provides a push notifications service and analytics, that's another point in favor.

We will proceed with creating a new account; after this, we need to name our application in Parse. Here, I will use `MasteringAndroid`. Once you name the application, you will be on the main page of your account. We need to navigate to **Data Service | Mobile | Android | Native Java**.

The following image shows the data services as a cloud:

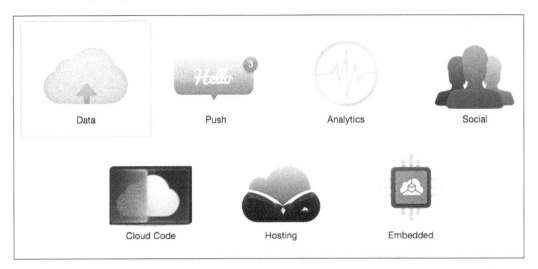

Adding the Parse SDK to our project

To access the data service from our app, we need to install the **Parse SDK (System Development Kit)**. For this, Parse refers us to a quick start guide, which contains all of the code, including the API Keys for our application, that is ready to be copied and pasted into our project.

Basically, we need to complete two steps:

1. The first one is to download a `.jar` library file that we need to copy into the `libs` folder in our project. After copying it, we need to tell our build system to include this library in our application. To do this, we need to find the `build.gradle` file inside our Application folder (be careful, there are two `build.gradle` files in our project) and add the following lines:

   ```
   dependencies {
     compile 'com.parse.bolts:bolts-android:1.+'
     compile fileTree(dir: 'libs', include: 'Parse-*.jar')
   }
   ```

2. In the following image, you can see the two files named `build.gradle`; the one that is selected is the right one:

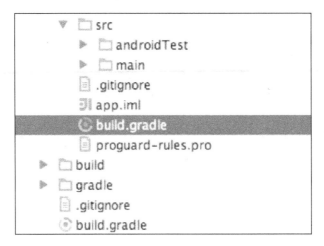

3. The second step is to initialize the Parse SDK in our project; for this, we can navigate directly to `https://www.parse.com/apps/quickstart?app_id=masteringandroidapp`. Replace your own app ID in the link or find the link by clicking on your home page, as in the following screenshot:

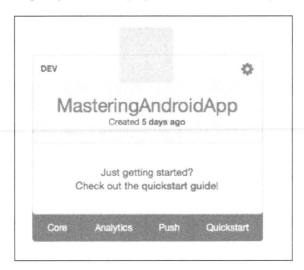

4. After clicking on **quickstart guide**, go to **Data | Mobile | Android | Native | Existing Project**.

5. It will ask you to add the `INTERNET` and `ACCESS_NETWORK_STATE` permissions to your `AndroidManifest.xml` file if they are not already added.

Android's Application class

The next thing we can take note of is that we need to add the code to initialize Parse to our `Application` class; however, our `Application` class is not created by default in our project. We need to create and understand what the `Application` class is and how it works.

To create an Application class, we will right-click on our package and create a new Java class called `MAApplication` extending `Application`. Once this extends `Application`, we can override the `onCreate` method. Then, we will right-click inside our **class | Generate. | Override Methods | onCreate**.

This will override the `onCreate` method, and we will be ready to implement our own functionality there. The `onCreate` method is called every time our `Application` is created; therefore, it's the right place to initialize our libraries and third-party SDKs. Now, you can copy and paste the Parse initialization lines as seen in quick start guide:

 Be careful, this is unique, and for your own account you should have your own keys.

```
Parse.initialize(this, "yourKeyHere", "yourKeyHere");
```

To finish, we need to tell our app that we have a new `Application` class and that that's the one we want to use; if we don't do this, our `Application` class won't be recognized and `onCreate` won't be called.

In our manifest, inside the `<application>` tag, we need to set the attribute name to match our own application. Execute the following code:

```
<application
    android:name="MApplication "
    android:icon="@drawable/ic_launcher"
    android:label="@string/app_newname"
>
```

The Application class encapsulates everything in our app; the activities are contained in the application, and subsequently, the fragments are contained in the **Activities**. If we need a global variable in our app that needs to be accessed by all Activities/ Fragments, this would be the right place to have it. In the next chapter, we will see how we can create this global variable. The following diagram is the graphic structure of an app:

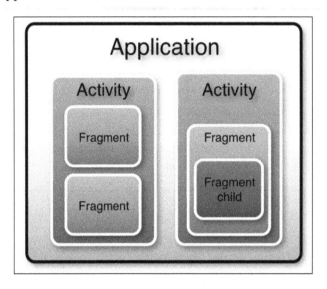

Creating the database

As we know, the example that we will create during this book is an app that will have Android-related job offers; therefore, we need to create a database to store these job offers.

The database can be changed during development (this will be more difficult to do when the app is released and has users). However, for now we will look at the big picture, creating the whole system rather than having a final version of the database with all the fields completed.

To create a table, click on the **Core** section as shown in the following screenshot:

First, create a table by clicking on the **+ Add Class** button and call it **JobOffer** with the following attributes, which can be added by clicking on the **Col+** button:

- `objectId`: This is created by default: `String`
- `title`: This is the job title: `String`
- `description`: This is the job description: `String`
- `salary`: This indicates the salary or daily rate: `String`
- `company`: This indicates the company offering the job: `String`
- `type`: This indicated the type of employee, which is permanent, contract, or freelancer: `String`
- `imageLink`: This is the image of the company: `String`.
- `Location`: This indicates the location of the job: `String`
- `createdAt` , `updatedAt`: This is the date of the job; the columns are created with a default date

To add data to the tables, select the table on the left and click on **+ Row**. We only need to complete the columns that we created; the columns created by default, such as the ID or date, will be completed automatically. So far, our table should look as follows:

Feel free to add more details, such as the contact person, e-mail, and mobile number. You could also add more tables; for instance, a new `JobType` table containing the type of job and the field type instead of `String` would be `Relation<JobType>`.

We have what we need for our example; the next thing to do is consume this data using our app.

Storing and consuming content from Parse

Parse is a very powerful tool that allows us to not only consume content very easily but also to store content in the cloud database from our device, which is a tedious task to do using the traditional method.

For example, if we wanted to upload an image to a custom server from our device, we would have to create a POST request and send a form with the right encoding, while attaching the picture as a FileBody object in MultiPartEntity and importing the Apache HTTP libraries:

```
HttpClient httpclient = new DefaultHttpClient();
HttpPost httppost = new HttpPost("URL TO SERVER");

MultipartEntity mpEntity = new MultipartEntity(HttpMultipartMode.
BROWSER_COMPATIBLE);
File file = new File(filePath);
mpEntity.addPart("imgField", new FileBody(file, "application/octet"));

httppost.setEntity(mpEntity);
HttpResponse response = httpclient.execute(httppost);
```

Now, let's have a look at the Parse alternative:

```
ParseFile imgFile = new ParseFile ("img.png", ImgByteArray);

ParseObject myParseObject = new ParseObject ("ParseClass");
 myParseObject.put("imageField", imgFile);
 myParseObject.saveInBackground();
```

Let's not forget error handling on Parse. In a very elegant way, you can simply write:

```
imageObj.saveInBackground(new SaveCallback() {
  @Override
  public void done(ParseException e) {
    if (e == null) {
      //Successful
    } else {
      //Error
    }
  }
});
```

Storing content

To elaborate on the simplicity of Parse, we will upload job offers to our Parse Cloud from our app.

To achieve this, we can create a button inside Contact Fragment, which we will set to invisible in the final version of the app as we don't want the users to upload job offers themselves.

With this button, we will create `ParseObject`, which is similar to a map. We will add the fields that we want to complete, and after this we will call the `saveInBackground()` method, which is the method that will upload the object. Execute the following code:

```
view.findViewById(R.id.addJobOffer).setOnClickListener(new View.
OnClickListener() {
  @Override
  public void onClick(View view) {

    ParseObject jobOffer = new ParseObject("JobOffer");

    jobOffer.put("title", "Android Contract");
    jobOffer.put("description", "6 months rolling   contract. /n The
client" +
    "is a worldwide known digital agency");
    jobOffer.put("type", "Contract");
    jobOffer.put("salary", "450 GBP/day");
    jobOffer.put("company", "Recruiters LTD");
    jobOffer.put("imageLink", "http://.....recruitersLTD_logo.png");
    jobOffer.put("location","Reading, UK");

    jobOffer.saveInBackground();
  }
});
```

If, in your own version of `MasteringAndroidApp`, you want the user to upload content, you could display a dialog with `EditText` for every field so that the user can write the job offer, press upload, and have you send the `jobOffer` object with the fields written by the user.

Run the app, navigate to **Contact**, and click on the button. If the data is uploaded correctly, upon opening the Parse Cloud database in a browser, you should see an extra row with the job offer just uploaded.

Remember to add the permissions in `AndroidManifest.xml`, `android.permission.ACCESS_NETWORK_STATE`, and `android.permission.INTERNET`.

Consuming content

Our objects in the Parse Cloud have an object identifier by default; it is the `objectId` field. Let's start retrieving an object by the ID, and after this, we can retrieve a list of all the objects with and without filters. Run the following code:

```
ParseQuery<ParseObject> query = ParseQuery.getQuery("JobOffer");
query.getInBackground("yourObjectID", new GetCallback<ParseObject>() {
  public void done(ParseObject object, ParseException e) {
    if (e == null) {
      // object will be our job offer
    } else {
      // something went wrong
    }
  }
});
```

The `ParseQuery` object will perform a query over the network asynchronously when the network request is finished. The method; `done (the ParseObject object, ParseException e)`, which is included in the callback, will be executed.

A good way to test the result is to print a log; in cases where the exception is `null`, it means that everything is okay.

```
if (e == null) {
  Log.d("PARSE_TEST",object.getString("Title"));
} else {
  // something went wrong
}
```

We could extract every field from `ParseObject` and create a `JobOffer` class in our app with a constructor whose parameters match the fields of the object. Use the following snippet:

```
JobOffer myJobOffer = new JobOffer(object.getString("title"), object.getString("description"), … );
```

However, there is a better way to do this. We can create a `JobOffer` class that extends `ParseObject` and where all fields will be automatically converted into variables in our class. This way, we can use our own class in a very convenient way instead of `ParseObject`:

```java
public void done(JobOffer jobOffer, ParseException e)
```

Don't forget to add the `@ParseClassName("Name")` annotation at the top of the class to let Parse know which object from the Cloud we want to instantiate and to register the subclass before initiating parse in `MAApplication`:

```java
public class MAApplication extends Application {


    @Override
    public void onCreate() {
        super.onCreate();

        // Enable Local Datastore.
        Parse.enableLocalDatastore(this);

        ParseObject.registerSubclass(JobOffer.class);

        Parse.initialize(this, "KEY", "KEY");
    }

}

@ParseClassName("JobOffer")
public class JobOffer extends ParseObject {

    public JobOffer() {
        // A default constructor is required.
    }

    public String getTitle() {
        return getString("title");
    }

    public void setTitle(String title) {
        put("title", title);
    }
```

```java
public String getDescription() {
    return getString("description");
}

public void setDescription(String description) {
    put("description", description);
}

public String getType() {
    return getString("type");
}

public void setType(String type) {
    put("type", type);
}
//Continue with all the fields..

}
```

Now that we have our custom class created, it's even easier to get a list with all the job offers. If we want, we can filter it with a parameter. For instance, I could retrieve all the permanent jobs with the following query:

```java
ParseQuery< JobOffer > query = ParseQuery.getQuery("JobOffer");
query.whereEqualTo("type", "Permanent");
query.findInBackground(new FindCallback<JobOffer>() {
    public void done(List<JobOffer> jobsList, ParseException e) {
        if (e == null) {
            Log.d("score", "Retrieved " + jobsList.size() + " jobs");
        } else {
            Log.d("score", "Error: " + e.getMessage());
        }
    }
});
```

Displaying content

Once the list of objects is retrieved, it is possible to create ListView and an Adapter that receives the objects as the parameters. To finish with Parse, we will use another feature that allows us to create an adapter directly from the result of the query; so, we don't have to create an Adapter class ourselves.

In both cases, we need to create ListView and view for the rows of the list. For now, just displaying the title and the first line of the description will do. We will customize this and add an image in *Chapter 7, Image Handling and Memory Management.* Create a row_job_offer.xml layout as follows:

```xml
<?xml version="1.0" encoding="utf-8"?>
<LinearLayout xmlns:android="http://schemas.android.com/apk/res/
android"
    android:orientation="vertical" android:layout_width="match_parent"
    android:layout_height="wrap_content"
    android:padding="10dp">


    <TextView
        android:id="@+id/rowJobOfferTitle"
        android:layout_width="fill_parent"
        android:layout_height="wrap_content"
        android:text="Title"
        android:textColor="#555"
        android:textSize="18sp"
        />

    <TextView
        android:id="@+id/rowJobOfferDesc"
        android:layout_marginTop="5dp"
        android:layout_width="fill_parent"
        android:layout_height="wrap_content"
        android:text="Description"
        android:textColor="#999"
        android:textSize="16sp"
        android:maxLines="1"
        android:ellipsize="marquee"
        />

</LinearLayout>
```

We are now ready to create `ParseQueryAdapter` and customize the `getItemView()` method. The huge advantage of this adapter is that we don't need to download data with a query because it is automatically done; basically, we can show a list of items from the cloud creating an adapter. It has never been so easy!

To override a method from a class — in this case, we want to override `getItemView` — we could create a subclass, a `MyQueryAdapter` class that extends `ParseQueryAdapter` and overrides the method inside this subclass. This is a good solution, especially if we want to instantiate the object more than once in our app.

However, there is a way to override methods from a class without having to extend it; we can add { } after the object instantiation. For instance, refer to the following code:

```
Object object = new Object() {

  //Override methods here

}
```

Using this approach, I can create a new `ParseQueryAdapter` and customize `getItemView`, as in the following code:

```
ParseQueryAdapter<JobOffer> parseQueryAdapter = new ParseQueryAdapter<
JobOffer>(getActivity(),"JobOffer") {

  @Override
  public View getItemView(JobOffer jobOffer, View v, ViewGroup parent)
{

    if (v == null) {
      v = View.inflate(getContext(), R.layout.row_job_offer, null);
    }

    super.getItemView(jobOffer, v, parent);

    TextView titleTextView = (TextView) v.findViewById(R.
id.rowJobOfferTitle);
    titleTextView.setText(jobOffer.getTitle());
    TextView descTextView = (TextView) v.findViewById(R.
id.rowJobOfferDesc);
    descTextView.setText(jobOffer.getDescription());

    return v;
  }

};
```

We will now create `ListView` in the layout of our `ListFragment`, find this view in `OnCreateView`, set the adapter to the list, and that's all. No more code is needed to retrieve the items and display them. If your list is empty, ensure that you import `com.packtpub.masteringandroidapp.fragments.ListFragment;` instead of `android.support.v4.app.ListFragment` in `MyPagerAdapter`; they are different objects, and using the latter would lead to an empty android built-in `ListFragment` being displayed.

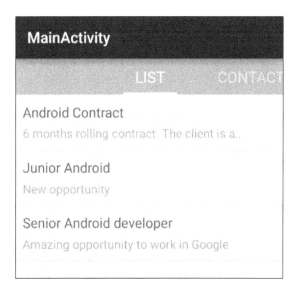

Google Volley and OkHttp

To master Android, we can't depend on a solution such as Parse. As developers, we must be prepared to face different server-side solutions. We can't always work with `ParseObjects` because we need to be able to do an HTTP `Post` request and consume the data in the JSON or XML format. However, this doesn't mean that we have to do all of this manually; we can use Google's official libraries to help us with parsing the data and the network requests.

For this, we will take a look at **Google Volley**, a powerful library, to manage our network requests. We will also discuss **OkHttp**, an ultrafast HTTP client, and combining the two them to get an amazing solution for network requests.

Google Volley

According to the official definition and list of features from `https://developer.` `android.com/training/volley/index.html`, *"Volley is an HTTP library that makes networking for Android apps easier and, most importantly, faster"*.

Volley offers the following benefits:

- Automatic scheduling of network requests
- Multiple concurrent network connections
- A transparent disk and memory response caching with a standard HTTP cache coherence
- Support for request prioritization
- Cancellation of request API; this means that you can cancel a single request, or set blocks or scopes of requests to cancel
- Ease of customization; for example, for retry and backoff
- Strong ordering, which makes it easy to correctly populate your UI with data fetched asynchronously from the network
- Debugging and tracing tools

Before Volley was born, managing network requests in Android was a hard task. Almost every application performs network requests. Features such as customizing retries — in case a connection fails and we need to try again — and managing concurrent network connections usually needed to be implemented manually by the developer. Nowadays, we are used to these kinds of libraries, but if we think about the situation some years ago, Volley is an excellent solution to this problem.

Before taking a look at how to create a request, we need to understand the concept of the Volley request queue object, `RequestQueue`. Every request performed by Volley must be added to this queue in order for it to be executed. The idea behind this is to have one single request queue in our application where all the network requests can be added and accessed by us from any part of our app. We will see how we can have an instance of an object that can be accessed globally in, *Chapter 4, Concurrency and Software Design Patterns*. Take a look at the following request:

```
// Instantiate the RequestQueue.
RequestQueue queue = Volley.newRequestQueue(this);
```

This request queue will use the following `HttpURLConnection` or `AndroidHttpClient` methods only if the Android version of the device is later than Gingerbread; `HttpURLConnection` is unreliable in versions earlier than Gingerbread.

```
// If the device is running a version >= Gingerbread...
if (Build.VERSION.SDK_INT >= Build.VERSION_CODES.GINGERBREAD) {
    // ...use HttpURLConnection for stack.
} else {
    // ...use AndroidHttpClient for stack.
}
```

When the request queue is instantiated, we just need to add a request to it. For instance, a network requests `https://www.google.com`, which logs the response:

```
String url ="https://www.google.com";

// Request a string response from the provided URL.
StringRequest stringRequest = new StringRequest(Request.Method.GET,
url,
            new Response.Listener<String>() {
    @Override
    public void onResponse(String response) {
        // Display the first 500 characters of the response string.
        Log.d("Volley","Response is: "+ response.substring(0,500));
    }
}, new Response.ErrorListener() {
    @Override
    public void onErrorResponse(VolleyError error) {
        Log.d("Volley","That didn't work!");
    }
});

// Add the request to the RequestQueue.
queue.add(stringRequest);
```

The request will be performed, and the `onResponse`(...) or `onErrorResponse`(...) method will be called in the application main thread, also known as the UI thread. We will explain the threads in Android in more detail in *Chapter 4, Concurrency and Software Design Patterns*.

OkHttp

OkHttp is an HTTP and SPDY client for Android and Java from the company, Square. It is not an alternative to Volley as it doesn't include a request queue. In fact, we could use OkHttp as an underlying layer for Volley, as we will see in the next section.

According to the official definition, "*HTTP is the way modern applications network. It's how we exchange data and media. Doing HTTP efficiently makes your stuff load faster and saves bandwidth*".

If we don't need to handle requests in a queue, prioritize requests, or schedule requests, we could use OkHttp directly in our app; we don't necessarily need Volley.

For example, the following method prints the contents of a response from a given URL:

```
OkHttpClient client = new OkHttpClient();

String run(String url) throws IOException {

  Request request = new Request.Builder()
      .url(url)
      .build();

  Response response = client.newCall(request).execute();
  return response.body().string();

}
```

Apart from being an easier way to do the requests than using `AsyncTask` or `HttpUrlConnection`, what convinces us to use OkHttp is the SPDY (speedy) protocol, which processes, tokenizes, simplifies, and compresses HTTP requests.

A lightning-fast network

If we want to keep the features of Volley to be able to have a flexible and manageable queue of requests and have quicker connections using the protocol SPDY, we can combine Volley and OkHttp.

This is really easy to do; while instantiating the request queue, we can specify which `HttpStack` method we want:

```
RequestQueue queue = Volley.newRequestQueue(this, new OkHttpStack());
```

Here, `OkHttpStack` is a class that we will create ourselves by extending `HurlStack`, which will use `OkUrlFactory`. This `OkUrlFactory` will open a URL connection; this will be done internally and there is no need to override the `createConnection` method:

```java
/**
 * An HttpStack subclass
 * using OkHttp as transport layer.
 */
public class OkHttpStack extends HurlStack {

    private final OkUrlFactory mFactory;

    public OkHttpStack() {
        this(new OkHttpClient());
    }

    public OkHttpStack(OkHttpClient client) {
        if (client == null) {
            throw new NullPointerException("Null client.");
        }
        mFactory = new OkUrlFactory(client);
    }
}
```

JSON and Gson

As an Android developer, sooner or later you will have to work with network requests in the JSON format. In some cases, you may also find XML, which makes it more tedious to translate to an object. It is important to know how to perform a network request by sending parameters in JSON and also how to consume data in the JSON format.

JSON and GSON are two different things; we need to understand the difference. JSON, or JavaScript Object Notation, is an open standard format that uses human-readable text to transmit data objects consisting of attribute–value pairs. It is used primarily to transmit data between a server and web application as an alternative to XML. This is an example of a JSON file; as you can see, we can have different types of attributes, and we can have nested JSON structures:

```json
{
  "firstName": "Antonio",
  "lastName": "Smith",
  "isDeveloper": true,
  "age": 25,
  "phoneNumbers": [
    {
      "type": "home",
      "number": "212 555-1234"
    },
    {
      "type": "office",
      "number": "646 555-4567"
    }
  ],
  "children": [],
  "spouse": null
}
```

Following are two examples of sending a network request with parameters as JSON. These examples cover Volley and OkHttp, which we discussed earlier in this chapter:

```java
//With Volley

public void post(String param1, String param2, String url) {

    Map<String, String> params = new HashMap<String, String>();
    params.put("param1",param1);
    params.put("param2",param2);

    JsonObjectRequest stringRequest = new  JsonObjectRequest(Request.
Method.POST, url, new JSONObject(params),  new Response.
Listener<JSONObject>() {

        @Override
        public void onResponse(JSONObject responseJSON) {

        }, new Response.ErrorListener() {
```

```java
    @Override
    public void onErrorResponse(VolleyError error) {
    }
  });



  // Add the request to the RequestQueue.
  requestQueue.add(stringRequest);
}


//With OkHttp

public static final MediaType JSON
= MediaType.parse("application/json; charset=utf-8");

String post(String url, String json) throws IOException {
  RequestBody body = RequestBody.create(JSON, json);
  Request request = new Request.Builder()
  .url(url)
  .post(body)
  .build();
  Response response = client.newCall(request).execute();
  return response.body().string();

}

//To create a JSONObject from a string

JSONObject responseJSON = new JSONObject(String json);
```

Gson (Google Gson) is an open source Java library used to serialize and deserialize Java objects to (and from) JSON.

If we were downloading the job offers for our application from a custom server in JSON, it would be in the following format:

```json
{
  "title": "Senior Android developer",
  "description": "A developer is needed for…",
  "salary": "25.000 € per year",
  .
  .
  .
}
```

Again, we don't want to create a new object manually and set all the parameters by retrieving them from JSON; what we want to do is create a `JobOffer` object from JSON. This is called **deserialization**.

To use this, we need to import the GSON library as a dependency in `build.gradle`:

```
dependencies {
compile 'com.google.code.gson:gson:2.2.4'
}
```

Gson has the `fromJSON` and `toJSON` methods to serialize and deserialize, respectively. The `fromJson` method takes the JSON code to convert, and the class of the object that we want it to be converted into, as the input. Use the following code:

```
Gson gson = new Gson();
JobOffer offer = gson.fromJson(JSONString, JobOffer.class);
```

If instead of a single object we had a list, which is the typical scenario while requesting data, we would need an extra step to get the type:

```
Gson gson = new Gson();
Type listType = new TypeToken<List<JobOffer>>(){}.getType();
List<JobOffer> listOffers = gson.fromJson(JSONString, listType);
```

To finish, if we want the fields in our class to have a different name than the fields of the JSON code to be deserialized, we can use annotations as follows:

```
import com.google.gson.annotations.SerializedName;

public class JobOffer extends ParseObject {

    @SerializedName("title")
    private String title;

    @SerializedName("description")
    private String desc;

    @SerializedName("salary")
    private String salary;
```

Summary

At the end of this chapter, you should be able to create your own database in Parse and consume content from the application. You should also have all the necessary knowledge to master network requests using Volley and OkHttp, especially while performing network requests and exchanging data in the JSON format.

In the next chapter, we will explain in further detail, some of the patterns used in this chapter for the HTTP libraries. For instance, we will understand what a callback is and which pattern it follows, as well as other commonly used software patterns in Android.

4
Concurrency and Software Design Patterns

As a developer, you not only have to write code that works, but also to use existing solutions whenever possible so that you can maintain your code better in the future. If other developers ever have to work on your project, they will quickly understand what you are doing. We can achieve this thanks to software design patterns.

In order to understand the patterns correctly, we need a basic overview of how concurrency works in Android. We will clarify what a UI thread is and talk about the different mechanisms used to delay events in a thread.

We will cover the most commonly used patterns in Android, which will help us further understand Android features and development techniques and become better developers.

- Concurrency
  - Handlers and threads
  - AsyncTask
  - Service
  - IntentService
  - Loader

- Patterns in Android
  - Singleton
  - Adapter and holder
  - Observer

Concurrency in Android

If you are an Android user, you are probably aware of ANR messages. It might not ring a bell for you, so take a look at the following image:

Activity Not Responding (ANR) happens when there is code running in the UI or main thread that blocks user interaction for more than 5 seconds.

In Android, an application runs a single thread, called the User Interface thread. We will explain what a thread is in a way that even readers with no programming background will understand. We can visualize a thread as a column of instructions or messages executed by the CPU. These instructions come from different places; they come from our application as well as the OS. This thread is used to handle the response from the user, lifecycle methods, and system callbacks.

The CPU processes messages sequentially, one after another; if it's busy, the message will wait in a queue to be executed. Therefore, if we perform long operations in our application and send many messages to the CPU, we will not let UI messages be executed, and this will result in the mobile not responding for the user.

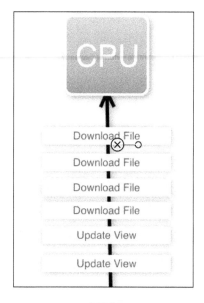

The solution to this problem seems obvious: if one thread isn't enough, we can use more than one. For instance, if we make a network request, this will be done in another thread, and when it finishes, it will communicate with the main thread to display the data that was requested.

Only the main or UI thread can access the UI; so, if we perform any background calculations in another thread, we have to tell the main thread to display the result of these calculations because we can't do it directly from there.

Handlers and threads

The messages that we have described previously run in a queue called `MessageQueue`, which is unique to each thread. A handler can send messages to this queue. When we create a handler, it is associated with the `MessageQueue` of the thread where it is created.

A handler is used for two situations:

- Sending a delayed message to the same thread
- Sending a message to another thread

This is why, in our `SplashActivity`, we will use the following code:

```
new Handler().postDelayed(new Runnable() {
  @Override
  public void run() {

    Intent intent = new Intent(SplashActivity.this, MainActivity.
class)

    startActivity(intent),
  }
},3000);
```

 When you create a new `Handler()` method, ensure that you import the `Android.OS` handler.

Here, we used the `postDelayed(Runnable, time)` method to send a message with a delayed time. In this case, the message is a runnable object that represents a command than can be executed.

When there is a method inside the `runOnUIThread()` activity that allows us to send a runnable object to the UI thread, you don't need to create a handler to communicate with it. This is very useful when we have the context of the activity and want to run something on the UI, for example posting updates to the UI from a task that's being executed in the background.

If we look at the Android source code of the method, we can see that it simply uses a handler to post the runnable object in the UI thread:

```
public final void runOnUiThread(Runnable action) {
  if (Thread.currentThread() != mUiThread) {
    mHandler.post(action);
  } else {
    action.run();
  }
}
```

Usually, threads are manually created when we want to perform a long task in the background and want to manage parallel thread executions. Threads have a `run()` method where the instructions are executed and must be started after its creation in order to start executing `run()`:

```
Thread thread = new Thread(){

  @Override
  public void run() {
    super.run();
  }
};

thread.start();
```

The drawback of creating threads and handlers to perform background tasks is its manual handling, and if we have many of them, we could easily end up with an application that is impossible to read. Android has other mechanisms to perform tasks, such as `AsyncTask`.

Introducing AsyncTasks

This is probably something you saw at the beginner level, but we will take a look at it from the concurrency perspective. An `Asynctask` is based on a thread and a handler and is meant to be an easy way to perform a job in the background and post UI updates.

An `AsyncTask` needs to be subclassed to be used, and it has four methods that can be overridden: `onPreExecute`, `doInBackground`, `onProgressUpdate`, and `onPostExecute`.

The `OnPreExecute` method is called before doing any work in the background; this means that it's still on the UI thread and is used to initialize variables and progress before starting the task.

The `doInBackground` method is executed in the background thread. Here, you can call `onProgressUpdate`, which posts an update to the UI thread, for instance, by increasing the value of `ProgressBar` to display the progress of the task.

The last method, `onPostExecute`, is called when the background task is finished and is running on the UI thread.

Let's consider as an example: an `AsyncTask` that takes x seconds to be completed in the background, updating the progress every second. The progress bar object is sent as a parameter in the constructor, and the number of seconds is sent as a parameter in the execute method, which is retrieved in `doInBackground`. Note that in the following code, the `<Integer, Integer, Void>` types refer to the types of input parameters, progress update, and on-post execute, respectively:

```java
public class MyAsyncTask extends AsyncTask<Integer, Integer, Void> {

    ProgressBar pB;

    MyAsyncTask(ProgressBar pB) {
        this.pB = pB;
    }

    @Override
    protected void onPreExecute() {
        super.onPreExecute();
        pB.setProgress(0);
    }

    @Override
    protected void onProgressUpdate(Integer... values) {
        super.onProgressUpdate(values);
        pB.setProgress(values[0]);
    }

    @Override
    protected Void doInBackground(Integer... integers) {
```

```
    for (int i = 0; i < 10; i++) {
      try {
        Thread.sleep(1000);
      } catch (InterruptedException e) {
        e.printStackTrace();
      }
      onProgressUpdate(new Integer[]{i});
    }
    return null;
  }

  @Override
  protected void onPostExecute(Void o) {
    super.onPostExecute(o);
    Log.d("AsyncTask","Completed");
  }

}
```

Having created an `AsyncTask` class, here's how we can execute it:

```
new MyAsyncTask( progressBar ).execute(new Integer[]{10});
```

If we execute more than one `AsyncTask` at a time, they will run sequentially by default in versions from Android 3.0 onward. If we want to run them in parallel, we will have to create an executor and call `executeOnExecutor()` with the `THREAD_POOL_EXECUTOR` parameter.

As for limitations, we should mention that `AsyncTask` always has to be executed from the main thread and that you can't call `execute()` twice in the same object; therefore, they cannot loop.

Understanding services

An `AsyncTask` is ideal while downloading a file or performing any short operation where you want to notify the UI when the task is finished. However, there are situations in Android where you need to perform a very long task that might not need UI interaction. For instance, you can have an application that opens a socket (a direct channel) with the server to stream audio for a radio listening app.

A service will run even if the app is not on the screen; it runs in the background but uses the main thread by default. Therefore, if we want to perform long tasks, we need to create a thread inside the service. It has to be declared in the manifest, and it can also be used from another application if we declare it public.

As opposed to `AsyncTask`, services can be triggered from any thread; they are triggered with the `onStartService()` method and stopped with `onStopService()`.

Optionally, services could be bound to a component; once you bind the components, `onBind()` is called. When binding takes place, we have an interface available to the component to interact with the service.

A type of service – IntentService

`IntentService` is a subclass of `services` that can be triggered from an intent. It creates a thread and includes callbacks to know when the task is finished.

The idea behind `IntentService` is that if you don't need to run a task in parallel, it is easier to implement a service that receives intents and manages them sequentially with a notification when the job is done.

Services run constantly as we call `onStart`; however, `IntentService` is created but runs in small intervals, only from when it receives the intent and until it finishes the tasks.

As a real example, we can think of an application that needs to perform short tasks in the background when the app is not on the screen. This could be the case of a newsreader app that stores the news in your device to give you offline access to it. It could be an app from a newspaper that publishes articles daily, allowing users to read them when they are in a plane or in commute on a train without a network connection.

The idea would be that when the article is published, users receive a push notification while the app is in the background. This notification will trigger an intent to download the article so that without any extra user interaction, the article is there the next time they open the app.

Downloading the article is a small and repetitive task that needs to be done when the app is in the background, in a thread, and without the need to be in parallel, which is the perfect scenario for `IntentService`.

Introducing loaders

To finish with the concurrency section, we will have a quick overview of the `Loader` class. The purpose of a loader is to make it easier to asynchronously load data in an activity and, therefore, in a fragment. From Android 3.0 onward, every activity has `LoaderManager` to manage the loaders used in it. In an application based on fragment navigations, it is possible to perform background operations at the activity level even when you switch between fragments.

Loaders load data from a source; when this source changes, it automatically refreshes the information, which is why loaders are perfect to use with a database. For instance, once we connect the loader to a database, this database can be modified, and the change will be captured by the loader. This will allow us to refresh the UI, instantly reflecting the changes to the user.

In *Chapter 8*, *Databases and Loaders*, we will implement `CursorLoader` to query the database that we will create in `MasteringAndroidApp`.

The importance of patterns

When a software developer has to develop a feature or a component with a certain functionality, it can usually be done in different ways; it can be done with different code or with a different structure. It is very likely that the same problem has been solved by other developers so many times that the solution is abstracted from particular implementations and transformed into a pattern. Rather than invent the wheel again, it is preferable to know and implement these patterns.

When developing on Android, we use patterns every day even if we aren't aware of it. Most of the time, we use implementations of the patterns built in Android. For instance, when we want to perform a click on a button and set `OnClickListener` — in other words, wait for the `onClick()` method to be called — we use an observer pattern implementation. If we create a popup, `AlertDialog`, we use `AlertDialog.Builder`, which uses the `Builder` pattern. There are many examples, but what we want is to be able to implement these solutions to our own problems.

There are different types of patterns grouped in four categories, and these are some examples of the ones that we find while developing Android apps:

- Creation
    - Singleton
    - Builder
    - Factory method

- Behavioral
    - Observer
    - Strategy
    - Iterator

- Structural
  - ° Adapter
  - ° Façade
  - ° Decorator

- Concurrency
  - ° Lock
  - ° Scheduler
  - ° Read-write lock

To complete `MasteringAndroidApp`, we have to implement patterns from the first three groups. With respect to the fourth group (concurrency), we need to have an idea of concurrency in Android, but we will not implement a concurrency pattern ourselves.

Patterns are usually represented by UML diagrams.

According to Wikipedia (`http://en.wikipedia.org/wiki/Class_diagram`), *"in software engineering, a class diagram in the Unified Modeling Language (UML) is a type of static structure diagram that describes the structure of a system by showing the system's classes, their attributes, operations (or methods), and the relationships among objects"*.

The Singleton pattern

The software design pattern, Singleton, restricts the creation of an object to a single instance. The idea is to access this single object globally.

This pattern is implemented by creating the object if has not been created before or returning the existing instance if created. Following is the UML diagram:

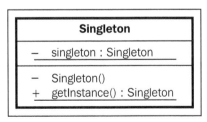

On certain occasions, we want an object to be globally accessible, and we want it to be unique in our app. For instance, while using Volley, we want to maintain a unique request queue to have all the requests in the same queue, and we want it to be accessed globally because we will need to add a request from any fragment or activity.

Here is a basic example of a singleton implementation:

```java
public class MySingleton {

    private static MySingleton sInstance;

    public static MySingleton getInstance(){
        if (sInstance == null) {
            sInstance = new MySingleton();
        }
        return sInstance;
    }
}
```

To understand the implementation, remember that in Java, a static variable is associated with the class and not with the object. In the same way, a static method can be called without creating an instance of the class.

Having a static method means that it can be called from anywhere in our app. We can call `MySingleton.getInstance()`, and it will always return the same instance. The first time, it will create it and return it; the subsequent times, it will return the one created.

There is a downside to using singleton and testing frameworks; we will talk about this in *Chapter 11, Debugging and Testing on Android*.

Singleton in the Application class

We can adapt a Singleton implementation to Android. Given that the `onCreate` method in the `Application` class is called only once when we open our app and that the `Application` object won't be destroyed, we can implement the `getInstance()` method in our application.

Upon applying these changes, our application class will look similar to the following:

```java
public class MAApplication extends Application {

    private static MAApplication sInstance;

    @Override
```

```
    public void onCreate() {
      super.onCreate();

      sInstance = this;

      // Enable Local Datastore.
      Parse.enableLocalDatastore(this);

      ParseObject.registerSubclass(JobOffer.class);

      Parse.initialize(this, "KEy", "KEY");
    }

    private static MAApplication getInstance(){
      return sInstance;
    }
  }
```

Now, I can call `MAAplication.getInstance()` from anywhere in the app and create member variables in the application class that can be accessed globally via the singleton `MAAplication` object. For instance, in the case of Volley, I can create `RequestQueue` in `OnCreate()` and then retrieve it at any time from the `MAAplication` object. Execute the following code:

```
  private RequestQueue mRequestQueue;

  @Override
  public void onCreate() {
    super.onCreate();

    sIntasnce = this;

    mRequestQueue = Volley.newRequestQueue(this);
      .
      .
      .
  }

  public RequestQueue getRequestQueue(){
    return mRequestQueue;
  }
```

Following this approach, we have one singleton, which is our `Application` class; the rest of the globally accessible objects are member variables. The other option is to create a new singleton class to store the volley requests queue and one new request singleton for every globally accessed object needed.

 Don't use this approach to persist data in the `Application` class. For example, if we go to the background by clicking on the home button, Android might need memory after a while and will kill the app. So, the next time you open the app, a new instance will be created even if it looks as though we are returning to the previous instance. This is fine if you initialize all the variables in `onCreate` again and don't modify their state later. Avoid having setters to ensure this.

The Observer pattern

This pattern is widely used in Android. Most of the network libraries that we discussed implement this pattern, and if you are an Android developer, you have surely used it plenty of times — we need to implement it even to detect a click on a button.

The observer pattern is based on an object, the observer, which registers other objects to notify them of a state change; here, the objects listening to the state changes are the *observers*. This pattern can be used to create a publish/subscribe system:

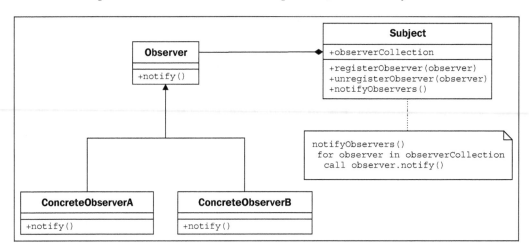

The following is an implementation of a pattern that registers multiple observes:

```java
public class MyObserved {

  public interface ObserverInterface{
    public void notifyListener();
  }

  List<ObserverInterface> observersList;

  public MyObserved(){
    observersList = new ArrayList<ObserverInterface>();
  }

  public void addObserver(ObserverInterface observer){
    observersList.add(observer);
  }

  public void removeObserver(ObserverInterface observer){
    observersList.remove(observer);
  }

  public void notifyAllObservers(){
    for (ObserverInterface observer : observersList){
      observer.notify();
    }
  }
}


public class MyObserver
implements MyObserved.ObserverInterface {

  @Override
  public void notify(){
    //Do something
  }
}
```

The observer, as you will notice, can be any object that implements the interface—
ObserverInterface. This interface is defined in the observed object.

If we compare this to the way that we handle a click on a button in Android, we perform `myButton.setOnClickListener(observer)`. Here, we add an observer that waits for the click; this observer implements the `OnClick()` method, which is the method that notifies in our case.

Looking at Volley, when we create a network request, we have to specify two listeners as a parameter: `Response.Listener` and `Response.ErrorListener`, which call `onResponse()` and `onErrorResponse()`, respectively. This is a clear implementation of the observer pattern.

We will implement an example of a variant of the observer pattern, a publish/subscribe pattern, in *Chapter 6, CardView and Material Design*.

Introducing the Adapter pattern

The **Adapter** is an element that we use in Android while creating `ListView` or `ViewPager`, but it is also a well-known design pattern. We will take a look at the definition of both and their relationship.

On one hand, an Adapter as a design pattern is one that acts as a bridge between two incompatible interfaces. It allows two different interfaces to work together. It's the same concept as a real-world adapter, such as an SD card to micro SD card adapter, which allows two incompatible systems to work together. As the diagram shows, the adapter is called with the new required method, but internally, it calls the old method from the *adaptee*.

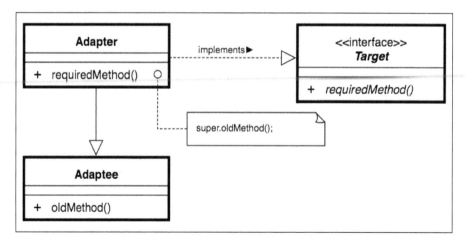

On the other hand, an Adapter from `android.widget.Adapter` is an object that we use to create the view for every row on a list or for every page in a view pager. Therefore, it adapts the data, a set of elements, and a set of views.

To implement an adapter, we have to extend `BaseAdapter` and override the `getView()` and `getCount()` methods. With these two methods, the adapter will know how many views it has to create and how the views are created.

We will go further into this topic in the next chapter while working with `ListViews`, and we will talk about the `ViewHolder` pattern, which is a particular pattern used in Android while working with Adapters and lists.

Summary

At the end of this chapter, you should be able to understand concurrency in Android and all the different mechanisms to work with it. You should know that there is a main thread where the UI is updated and that we can create background threads to perform other tasks. You must also know the difference between having the app perform a task in the background (in other words, not on the screen) and having the app perform tasks in a background thread. You should also know the importance of software design patterns and be able to implement some of them.

In the next chapter, we will take a look at how to work with list views, we will implement an adapter, and we will discover a new pattern, `ViewHolder`, which will be the key to understanding the difference between `ListView` and `RecyclerView` introduced in Android Lollipop.

5
Lists and Grids

In this chapter, we will work with lists and grids. A list or a matrix of elements can be found in almost every app on the market. Knowing how to display a list of elements on Android is something that you learn at a basic level; however, there is a lot to expand on and understand.

It's important to know which patterns we can use here, how to recycle the view, and how to display different kinds of elements with different views in the same list.

With this in mind, we will be able to understand why `RecyclerView` is the successor of `ListView`, and we will learn how to implement a list with this component. Therefore, we will cover the following in this chapter:

- Starting with lists
    - ListView
    - The custom adapter
    - Recycling views
    - Using the ViewHolder pattern

- Introducing RecyclerView
    - List, grid, or stack
    - Implementation

- OnItemClick

Starting with lists

If you have heard of `RecyclerView`, you might wonder why we are going through `ListView`. The `RecyclerView` widget is new; it came out with Android Lollipop, and is a revolution when displaying a list of items; it can do it vertically and horizontally, as a list or as a grid, or with nice animations among other improvements.

Answering the question, even if `RecyclerView` is more efficient and flexible in some scenarios, it needs extra coding to achieve the same result, so there are still reasons to use `ListView`. For example, there is no `onItemClickListener()` for item selection in `RecyclerView`, and there is no visual feedback when we click on an item. If we don't need customization and animations, for instance for a simple data picker popup, this could be a dialog where we just have to select a country. In this case, it's perfectly fine to use `ListView` rather than `RecyclerView`.

Another reason to start with `ListView` is that `RecyclerView` solves most of the problems presented when working with `ListViews`. Therefore, by starting with `ListView` and solving these problems, we will fully understand how `RecyclerView` works and why it is implemented this way. Thus, we will explain individually the patterns that are used to have a global idea of the component.

Here is an example of the basic `AlertDialog` with the purpose of selecting an item; here, the use of `ListView` makes perfect sense:

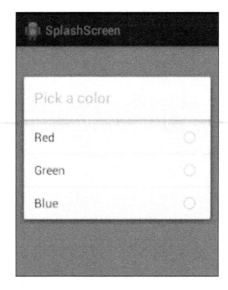

Using ListViews with built-in views

When you first implement `ListView`, it might seem trivial and easy; however, when you spend more time with Android, you realize how complex it can get. You can very easily find performance and memory issues by just having a large list of elements with an image on every row. It can be difficult to customize the list if you try to implement a complex UI; for example, having the same list displaying different items, creating different rows with different views, or even trying to group some items while showing a section title can be a headache.

Let's start with the shortest way to implement a list, using the Android built-in item layout, which is created to be used in simple lists as discussed before. In order to show the list, we will include it in `AlertDialog`, which will be shown when we tap on a button in the settings fragment. I will set the text of the button to `Lists Example`.

The first step is to create the button in `settings_fragment.xml`; once created, we can set the click listener to the button. Now, we understand a bit more about software patterns instead of setting the click listener in the following way:

```
view.findViewById(R.id.settingsButtonListExample).
setOnClickListener(new View.OnClickListener() {
  @Override
  public void onClick(View view) {
    //Show the dialog here
  }
});
```

We will do it in a more structured way, especially because we know that in the settings screen, there will be a good number of buttons, and we want to handle all the clicks in the same place. Instead of creating `onClickListener` inside the method call, we will make the `Fragment` implement `OnClikListener` by setting `onClickListener` to `this`. The `this` keyword refers to the whole fragment here, so the fragment will be listening for the click in the `onClick` method, which is mandatory to implement once the `Fragment` implements `View.OnClickListener`.

The `OnClick()` method receives a view, which is the view clicked on. If we compare that view's ID with the ID of the button, we will know whether the button or the other view where we set `clickListener` has been clicked.

Just type `implements View.OnClickListener` when defining the class, and you will be asked to implement the mandatory methods:

```
/**
 * Settings Fragment
 */
public class SettingsFragment extends Fragment implements View.
OnClickListener {


    @Override
    public View onCreateView(LayoutInflater inflater, ViewGroup
    container,
        Bundle savedInstanceState) {
        // Inflate the layout for this fragment
        View view = inflater.inflate(R.layout.fragment_settings,
    container, false);

        view.findViewById(R.id.settingsButtonListExample).
    setOnClickListener(this);

        view.findViewById(R.id.ViewX).setOnClickListener(this);

        view.findViewById(R.id.imageY).setOnClickListener(this);


        return view;
    }

    @Override
    public void onClick(View view) {
        switch (view.getId()){
            case (R.id.settingsButtonListExample) :
            showDialog();
            break;
            case (R.id.viewX) :
            //Example
            break;
            case (R.id.imageY) :
            //Example
            break;

            //...
        }
```

```
    }

    public void showListDialog(){
      //Show Dialog here
    }
  }
```

You will notice that we also move the logic to show the list dialog to an external method, keeping the structure easy to read in onClick();.

Continuing with the dialog, we can show an AlertDialog that has a setAdapter() property, which automatically binds the items with an internal ListView. Alternatively, we could create a view for our dialog with ListView on it and then set the adapter to that ListView:

```
/**
 *  Show a dialog with different options to choose from
 */
public void showListDialog(){

  AlertDialog.Builder builder = new AlertDialog.
Builder(getActivity());

  final ArrayAdapter<String> arrayAdapter = new ArrayAdapter<String>(
  getActivity(),
  android.R.layout.select_dialog_singlechoice);
  arrayAdapter.add("Option 0");
  arrayAdapter.add("Option 1");
  arrayAdapter.add("Option 2");

  builder.setTitle("Choose an option");

  builder.setAdapter(arrayAdapter,
  new DialogInterface.OnClickListener() {
    @Override
    public void onClick(DialogInterface dialogInterface, int i) {
      Toast.makeText(getActivity(),"Option choosen "+i, Toast.LENGTH_
SHORT).show();
      dialogInterface.dismiss();
    }
  });

  builder.show();
}
```

This dialog will show a message indicating the option clicked. We have used `android.R.layout.select_dialog_singlechoice` as a view for our rows.

These are a few different examples of built-in layouts for lists, which will depend on the theme of our application. The dialog won't look the same in 4.4 KitKat and in 5.0 Lollipop, for instance, in `android.R.layout.simple_list_item_1`, this is how it will look:

android.resource.id.text1

Here's what `android.R.layout.simple_list_item_2` with two rows will look similar to:

android.resource.id.text1

android.resource.id.text2

This is an example of `android.R.layout.simpleListItemChecked`, where we can change the choice mode to multiple or single:

android.resource.id.text1

This is `android.R.layout.activityListItem`, where we have an icon and text:

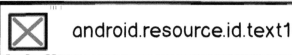

We can access these built-in layout components to tweak the view a bit more when creating the layout. These components are named `android.resource.id.Text1`, `android.resource.id.Text2`, `android.resource.id.Icon`, and so on.

Now, we have an idea of how to create lists with the functionality and views ready to be used. It's time to create our own Adapter and implement the functionality and the view manually.

Creating a custom Adapter

When you look for a job, apart from looking at offers, you would also be handing your CV to different software companies or to IT recruitment companies that will find a company for you.

In our contact fragment, we will create a list sorted by country, displaying the contact details of these companies. There will be two different rows: one for the country header and another one for the company details.

We can create another table in our Parse database, called `JobContact`, with the following fields:

We will request the job contacts from the server and build a list of items that will be sent to the Adapter to build the list. In the list, we will send two different elements: the company and the country. What we can do is generate a list of items and add the two as objects. Our two classes will look similar to the following:

```
@ParseClassName("JobContact")
public class JobContact extends ParseObject {

  public JobContact() {
    // A default constructor is required.
  }
```

```java
    public String getName() {
      return getString("name");
    }

    public String getDescription() {
      return getString("description");
    }

    public String getCountry() {
      return getString("country");
    }

    public String getEmail() {
      return getString("email");
    }

  }

  public class Country {

    String countryCode;

    public Country(String countryCode) {
      this.countryCode = countryCode;
    }

  }
```

Once we download the information sorted by country from `http://www.parse.com`, we can build our list of items, iterating through the parse list and adding a country header when a different country is detected. Execute the following code:

```java
public void retrieveJobContacts(){
  ParseQuery<JobContact> query = ParseQuery.getQuery("JobContact");
  query.orderByAscending("country");
  query.findInBackground(new FindCallback<JobContact>() {
    @Override
    public void done(List<JobContact> jobContactsList, ParseException
  e) {
```

```
        mListItems = new ArrayList<Object>();
        String currentCountry = "";
        for (JobContact jobContact: jobContactsList) {
          if (!currentCountry.equals(jobContact.getCountry())){
            currentCountry = jobContact.getCountry();
            mListItems.add(new Country(currentCountry));
          }
          mListItems.add(jobContact);
        }
      }
    });
}
```

Now that we have our list with the headers included we are ready to create the Adapter based on this list, which will be sent as a parameter in the constructor. The best way to customize an Adapter is to create a subclass extending BaseAdapter. Once we do this, we will be asked to implement the following methods:

```
public class JobContactsAdapter extends BaseAdapter {
  @Override
  public int getCount() {
    return 0;
  }

  @Override
  public Object getItem(int i) {
    return null;
  }

  @Override
  public long getItemId(int i) {
    return 0;
  }

  @Override
  public View getView(int i, View view, ViewGroup viewGroup) {
    return null;
  }
}
```

These methods will have to be implemented according to the data that we want to display; for instance, getCount() will have to return the size of the list. We need to implement a constructor receiving two parameters: the list and the context. The context will be necessary to inflate the list in the getView() method. This is how the adapter will look without implementing getView():

```java
public class JobContactsAdapter extends BaseAdapter {

  private List<Object> mItemsList;
  private Context mContext;

  public JobContactsAdapter(List<Object> list, Context context){
    mItemsList = list;
    mContext = context;
  }

  @Override
  public int getCount() {
    return mItemsList.size();
  }

  @Override
  public Object getItem(int i) {
    return mItemsList.get(i);
  }

  @Override
  public long getItemId(int i) {
    //Not needed
    return 0;
  }

  @Override
  public View getView(int i, View view, ViewGroup viewGroup) {
    return null;
  }
}
```

In our case, we can create two different views; so, apart from the mandatory methods, we need to implement two extra methods:

```
@Override
public int getItemViewType(int position) {
  return mItemsList.get(position) instanceof Country ? 0 : 1;
}

@Override
public int getViewTypeCount() {
  return 2;
}
```

The `getItemViewType` method will return 0 if the element is a country or 1 if the element is a company. With the help of this method, we can implement `getView()`. In case it's a country, we inflate `row_job_country.xml`, which contains `ImageView` and `TextView`; in case it's a company, we inflate `row_job_contact.xml`, which contains three text views:

```
@Override
public View getView(int i, View view, ViewGroup viewGroup) {

  View rowView = null;
  switch (getItemViewType(i)){

    case (0) :
    rowView = View.inflate(mContext, R.layout.row_job_country,null);
    Country country = (Country) mItemsList.get(i);
    ((TextView) rowView.findViewById(R.id.rowJobCountryTitle)).
setText(country.getName());
    ((ImageView) rowView.findViewById(R.id.rowJobCountryImage)).
setImageResource(country.getImageRes(mContext));
    break;

    case (1) :
    rowView = View.inflate(mContext, R.layout.row_job_contact,null);
    JobContact company = (JobContact) mItemsList.get(i);
    ((TextView) rowView.findViewById(R.id.rowJobContactName)).
setText(company.getName());
    ((TextView) rowView.findViewById(R.id.rowJobContactEmail)).
setText(company.getEmail());
    ((TextView) rowView.findViewById(R.id.rowJobContactDesc)).
setText(company.getDescription());
  }

  return rowView;
}
```

To finish, we can create `ListView` in `contact_fragment.xml` and set the adapter to this list. However, we will take a shortcut and use `android.support.v4.ListFragment`; this is a fragment that already inflates a view with `ListView` and contains the `setListAdapter()` method, which sets an adapter to the built-in `ListView`. Extending from this fragment, our `ContactFragment` class will look similar to the following code:

```
public class ContactFragment extends android.support.v4.app.
ListFragment {

  List<Object> mListItems;

  public ContactFragment() {
    // Required empty public constructor
  }

  @Override
  public void onViewCreated(View view, Bundle bundle) {
    super.onViewCreated(view,bundle);
    retrieveJobContacts();
  }

  public void retrieveJobContacts(){
    ParseQuery<JobContact> query = ParseQuery.getQuery("JobContact");
    query.orderByAscending("country");
    query.findInBackground(new FindCallback<JobContact>() {
      @Override
      public void done(List<JobContact> jobContactsList,
ParseException e) {
        mListItems = new ArrayList<Object>();
        String currentCountry = "";
        for (JobContact jobContact: jobContactsList) {
          if (!currentCountry.equals(jobContact.getCountry())){
            currentCountry = jobContact.getCountry();
            mListItems.add(new Country(currentCountry));
          }
          mListItems.add(jobContact);
        }
        setListAdapter(new JobContactsAdapter(mListItems,getActivi
ty()));
      }
    });
  }
}
```

Upon calling the `retrieveJobContacts()` method after the view has been created, we achieve the following result:

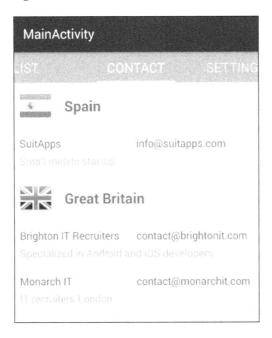

The flags that we have displayed are images in the `drawable` folder whose name matches the country code, *drawable/ "country_code" .png*. We can display them by setting the resource identifier to `ImageView` and retrieving it with the following method inside the `Country` class:

```
public int getImageRes(Context ctx){
   return ctx.getResources().getIdentifier(countryCode, "drawable",
ctx.getPackageName());
}
```

This is a basic version of `ListView` with two different types of rows. This version is still far from perfect; it lacks performance. It does not recycle the views, and it finds the IDs of the widget every time we create a row. We will explain and solve this problem in the following section.

Recycling views

While working with `ListView`, we need to keep in mind that the number of rows is a variable and we always want the list to feel fluent even if we scroll as quickly as we can. Hopefully, Android helps us a lot with this task.

When we scroll through `ListView`, the views that are not visible anymore on one side of the screen are reused and displayed again on the other side. This way, android saves inflation of the views; when it inflates, a view has to go through the xml nodes, instantiating every component. This extra computation can be the difference between a fluent and staggering list.

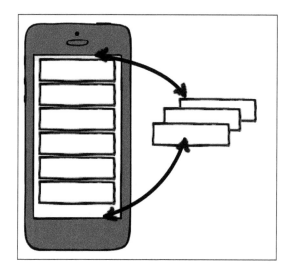

The `getView()` method receives as a parameter one of the views that are to be recycled or null if there are no views to be recycled.

To take advantage of this view recycling, we need to stop creating a view every time and reuse the view coming as a parameter. We still need to change the value of the text views and widget inside the row on a recycled view because it has the initial values that correspond to its previous position. In our example, we have an extra complication; we cannot recycle a country view to be used for a company view, so we can only recycle views of the same view type. However, again, Android does that check for us using internally the `getItemViewType` method that we implemented:

```
@Override
public View getView(int i, View view, ViewGroup viewGroup) {
```

```
        switch (getItemViewType(i)){

        case (0) :
        if (view == null){
            view = View.inflate(mContext, R.layout.row_job_country,null);
        }
        Country country = (Country) mItemsList.get(i);
        ((TextView) view.findViewById(R.id.rowJobCountryTitle)).
setText(country.getName());
        ((ImageView) view.findViewById(R.id.rowJobCountryImage)).
setImageResource(country.getImageRes(mContext));
        break;

        case (1) :
        if (view == null){
            view = View.inflate(mContext, R.layout.row_job_contact,null);
        }
        JobContact company = (JobContact) mItemsList.get(i);
        ((TextView) view.findViewById(R.id.rowJobContactName)).
setText(company.getName());
        ((TextView) view.findViewById(R.id.rowJobContactEmail)).
setText(company.getEmail());
        ((TextView) view.findViewById(R.id.rowJobContactDesc)).
setText(company.getDescription());
        }

    return view;
}
```

Applying the ViewHolder pattern

Note that in getView(), every time we want to set a text to TextView, we search this TextView in row view with the findViewById() method; even when the row is recycled, we still find the TextView again to set the new value.

We can create a class called ViewHolder, which holds the reference to the widget by saving the computation of the widget search inside the row. This ViewHolder class will only contain references to the widgets, and we can keep a reference between a row and its ViewHolder class through the setTag() method. A View object allows us to set an object as a tag and retrieve it later; we can add as many tags as we want by specifying a key for this tag: setTag(key) or getTag(key). If no key is specified, we can save and retrieve the default tag.

Following this pattern for the first time that we create the view, we will create the `ViewHolder` class and set it as a tag to the view. If the view is already created and we are recycling it, we will simply retrieve the holder. Execute the following code:

```
@Override
public View getView(int i, View view, ViewGroup viewGroup) {

    switch (getItemViewType(i)){

    case (0) :
    CountryViewHolder holderC;
    if (view == null){
        view = View.inflate(mContext, R.layout.row_job_country,null);
        holderC = new CountryViewHolder();
        holderC.name = (TextView) view.findViewById(R.
id.rowJobCountryTitle);
        holderC.flag = (ImageView) view.findViewById(R.
id.rowJobCountryImage);
        view.setTag(view);
    } else {
        holderC = (CountryViewHolder) view.getTag();
    }
    Country country = (Country) mItemsList.get(i);
    holderC.name.setText(country.getName());
    holderC.flag.setImageResource(country.getImageRes(mContext));
    break;
    case (1) :
    CompanyViewHolder holder;
    if (view == null){
        view = View.inflate(mContext, R.layout.row_job_contact,null);
        holder = new CompanyViewHolder();
        holder.name = (TextView) view.findViewById(R.
id.rowJobContactName);
        holder.email = (TextView) view.findViewById(R.
id.rowJobContactEmail);
        holder.desc = (TextView) view.findViewById(R.
id.rowJobOfferDesc);
        view.setTag(holder);
    } else {
        holder = (CompanyViewHolder) view.getTag();
    }
    JobContact company = (JobContact) mItemsList.get(i);
    holder.name.setText(company.getName());
```

```
     holder.email.setText(company.getEmail());
     holder.desc.setText(company.getDescription());
   }

   return view;
}

private class CountryViewHolder{

   public TextView name;
   public ImageView flag;

}

private class CompanyViewHolder{

   public TextView name;
   public TextView email;
   public TextView desc;

}
```

To simplify this code, we can create a method called bindView() inside each holder; it will get a country or company object and populate the widgets:

```
CountryViewHolder holderC;
if (view == null){
   view = View.inflate(mContext, R.layout.row_job_country,null);
   holderC = new CountryViewHolder(view);
   view.setTag(view);
} else {
   holderC = (CountryViewHolder) view.getTag();
}
holderC.bindView((Country)mItemsList.get(i));
break;



private class CountryViewHolder{

   public TextView name;
   public ImageView flag;
```

```
    public CountryViewHolder(View view) {
        this.name = (TextView) view.findViewById(R.id.rowJobCountryTitle);
        this.flag = (ImageView) view.findViewById(R.
id.rowJobCountryImage);
    }

    public void bindView(Country country){
        this.name.setText(country.getName());
        this.flag.setImageResource(country.getImageRes(mContext));
    }

}
```

We will now finish with the list of ListView performance improvements. If there are images or long operations to load a view, we need to create AsyncTask method inside getView() so as to avoid heavy operation while scrolling. For instance, if we want to display an image downloaded from the Internet on every row, we would have a LoadImageAsyncTask method, which we will execute with the holder and the URL to download the image from. When the Asynctask method finishes, it will have a reference to the holder and will therefore be able to display the image:

```
public View getView(int position, View convertView,
ViewGroup parent) {


    . . .


    new LoadImageAsyncTask(list.get(position).getImageUrl, holder)
    .executeOnExecutor(AsyncTask.THREAD_POOL_EXECUTOR, null);

    return convertView;
}
```

Now that we know all of the different techniques to improve the performance of a ListView, we are ready to introduce RecyclerView. By applying most of these techniques in the implementation, we will be able to identify it easily.

Introducing RecyclerView

The RecyclerView was introduced in Android 5.0 Lollipop and was defined by Google as a more flexible and advanced version of ListView. It is based on an Adapter class similar to ListView, but it enforces the use of a ViewHolder class to improve performance and modularity, as we have seen in the previous section. The flexibility comes in when we decouple the item representation from the component and allow animations, item decorations, and layout managers to do the work.

The RecyclerView handles the adding and removing of animations using RecyclerView.ItemAnimator, which we can subclass to customize the animations. If you display data from a source or if the data changes, for instance by adding or removing items, you can call notifyItemInserted() or notifyItemRemoved() to trigger the animations.

To add separators, group items, or highlight an item, we can use RecyclerView. ItemDecoration.

One of the main differences in utilizing ListView is the use of layout managers to position the items. With ListView, we know that our items will always be displayed vertically, and if we want to have a grid, we can use GridView. Layout managers make our list more flexible in that we can display elements as we want and can even create our own layout manager.

Using list, grid, or stack

By default, we have three built-in layout managers: LinearLayoutManager, GridLayoutManager, and StaggeredLayoutManager.

The LinearLayoutManager displays the items aligned in a list, where we can specify the orientation—vertical or horizontal.

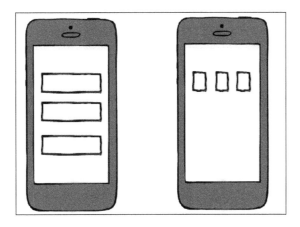

The `GridLayoutManager` displays the items as a matrix, where we can specify the columns and rows:

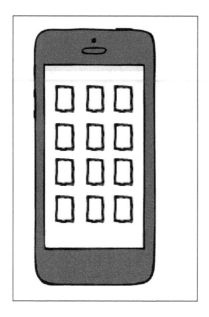

The `StaggereGriddLayoutManager` displays the items in a staggered way; these items can have different widths or heights, and we can control how they are displayed with `setGapStrategy()`.

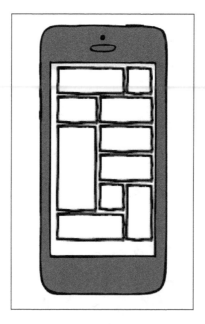

Implementing RecyclerView

Continuing with `MasteringAndroidApp`, we will implement again the list of job offers, removing `ParseQueryAdapter` and using `RecyclerView` instead. We will still query the data from Parse, but this time, what we will do is save the list of items in a variable and use it to build `RecyclerView.Adapter`, which will be used by `RecyclerView`.

The `RecyclerView` is included in the v7 support library; the best way to include it in our project is to open the project structure, click on the dependencies tab, and search for `RecyclerView`. A list of results will be presented as shown in the following screenshot:

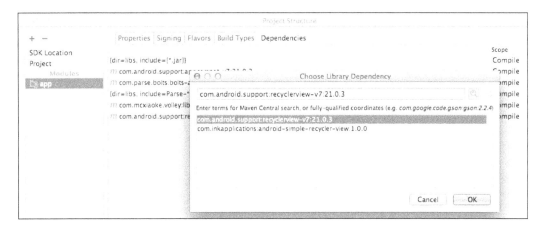

This is the equivalent of adding the following line to the `build.gradle` dependencies:

```
dependencies {
    compile fileTree(dir: 'libs', include: ['*.jar'])
    compile 'com.android.support:appcompat-v7:21.0.3'
    compile 'com.parse.bolts:bolts-android:1.+'
    compile fileTree(dir: 'libs', include: 'Parse-*.jar')
    compile 'com.mcxiaoke.volley:library-aar:1.0.1'
    compile 'com.android.support:recyclerview-v7:21.0.3'
}
```

Once the line is added, we will click on **Sync Gradle with Project files** to update the dependencies and get ready to use `RecyclerView` in our XML.

Open `fragment_list.xml` and replace the existing `ListView` with `RecyclerView`, as follows:

```xml
<android.support.v7.widget.RecyclerView
  android:id="@+id/my_recycler_view"
  android:scrollbars="vertical"
  android:layout_width="match_parent"
  android:layout_height="match_parent"/>
```

If you don't get any errors after adding it, the dependency was added correctly.

The next step is to create the adapter. This adapter is slightly different from the adapter that we created for the job contacts; instead of extending `BaseAdapter`, we will extend `RecyclerView.Adapter <RecyclerView.MyViewHolder>`, which is an adapter that implements the `ViewHolder` pattern after creating the `JobOfferAdapter` adapter class. However, before extending, we have to create an internal `MyViewHolder` class extending `RecylcerView.ViewHolder`. So far, we have the following code:

```java
public class JobOffersAdapter  {

    public class MyViewHolder extends RecyclerView.ViewHolder{

        public TextView textViewName;
        public TextView textViewDescription;

        public  MyViewHolder(View v){
            super(v);
            textViewName = (TextView)v.findViewById(R.id.rowJobOfferTitle);
            textViewDescription = (TextView)v.findViewById(R.
    id.rowJobOfferDesc);
        }
    }
}
```

Now is when we extend the `JobOffersAdapter` class from `RecyclerView.Adapter<JobsOfferAdapter.MyViewHolder>`. We will be asked to implement the following methods:

```java
@Override
public MyViewHolder onCreateViewHolder(ViewGroup parent, int viewType)
{
    return null;
}
```

```
@Override
public void onBindViewHolder(MyViewHolder holder, int position) {

}

@Override
public int getItemCount() {
  return 0;
}
```

Following the same approach as in JobsContactsAdapter, we create a constructor by receiving the list of job offers and implement the adapter methods based on that list.

OnBindViewHolder receives the holder with a position; all we need to do is get the job offer in that position on the list and update the holder text views with these values. OnCreateViewHolder will inflate the view; in this case, we only have one type, so we ignore the ViewType parameter. We will show here an alternative way to inflate the view: using the context of the parent, which comes as a parameter.

Finally, getItemCount will return the number of job offers. As you complete all of the above tasks, our new Adapter will be created with the following code:

```
public class JobOffersAdapter extends RecyclerView.
Adapter<JobOffersAdapter.MyViewHolder> {

  private  List<JobOffer> mOfferList;

  public JobOffersAdapter(List<JobOffer> offersList) {
    this.mOfferList = offersList;
  }

  @Override
  public MyViewHolder onCreateViewHolder(ViewGroup parent, int
viewType) {
    View v = LayoutInflater.from(parent.getContext()).inflate(R.
layout.row_job_offer, parent, false);
    return new MyViewHolder(v);
  }

  @Override
  public void onBindViewHolder(MyViewHolder holder, int position) {
    holder.textViewName.setText(mOfferList.get(position).getTitle());
    holder.textViewDescription.setText(mOfferList.get(position).
getDescription());
```

```
  }

  @Override
  public int getItemCount() {
    return mOfferList.size();
  }

  public class MyViewHolder extends RecyclerView.ViewHolder{

    public TextView textViewName;
    public TextView textViewDescription;

    public  MyViewHolder(View v){
      super(v);
      textViewName = (TextView)v.findViewById(R.id.rowJobOfferTitle);
      textViewDescription = (TextView)v.findViewById(R.
  id.rowJobOfferDesc);
      }
    }
  }
```

That is all that we need from the adapter side; now, we need to initialize
`RecyclerView` and set a layout manager along with the adapter. The adapter has to
be instantiated using the list of objects from Parse in the same way that we retrieved
our job contacts in the previous Adapter. First, in OnCreateView, we will initialize
RecyclerView:

```
public class ListFragment extends android.support.v4.app.Fragment {

  public List<JobOffer> mListItems;
  public RecyclerView mRecyclerView;

  public ListFragment() {
    // Required empty public constructor
  }

  @Override
  public View onCreateView(LayoutInflater inflater, ViewGroup
container,
  Bundle savedInstanceState) {
```

```
    // Inflate the layout for this fragment
    View view = inflater.inflate(R.layout.fragment_list, container,
false);

    mRecyclerView = (RecyclerView) view.findViewById(R.id.my_recycler_
view);

    // use this setting to improve performance if you know that
changes
    // in content do not change the layout size of the RecyclerView
    mRecyclerView.setHasFixedSize(true);

    // use a linear layout manager
    mRecyclerView.setLayoutManager(new LinearLayoutManager(getActivi
ty()));

    //Retrieve the list of offers
    retrieveJobOffers();

    return view;
}
```

In the end, we will call `retrieveOffers()`, which is an `async` operation. Only when the result is retrieved from Parse will we be able to create the adapter and set it to the list:

```
public void retrieveJobOffers(){

  ParseQuery<JobOffer> query = ParseQuery.getQuery("JobOffer");
  query.findInBackground(new FindCallback<JobOffer>() {

    @Override
    public void done(List<JobOffer> jobOffersList, ParseException e) {
      mListItems = jobOffersList;
      JobOffersAdapter adapter = new JobOffersAdapter(mListItems);
      mRecyclerView.setAdapter(adapter);
    }

  });
}
```

The best way to test all that we set to work is to see if there are any errors in the console. If all runs fine, you should be able to see the list of offers, as in the following screenshot:

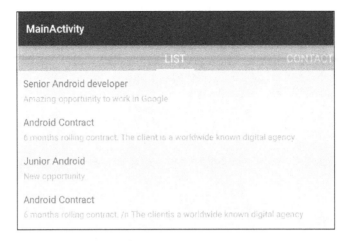

We have intentionally added a repeated job offer, which we will delete in order to see the removing animations included by default in RecyclerView. We will implement this functionality in a **long click listener**. The click listener is performed only to open the offer in the detail view. We will see how to do this in the next section.

Clicking on RecyclerView items

In ListView, it was quite easy to detect a click on an item; we could simply perform ListView.setOnItemClickLister and setOnItemLongClickListener for long clicks. However, this implementation is not as quick with RecyclerView; the flexibility comes at a cost.

There are two approaches to implementing an item click here: one is to create a class that implements RecyclerView.OnItemTouchListener and calls the RecyclerView method, addOnItemTouchListener, as follows:

```
mrecyclerView.addOnItemTouchListener(new MyRecyclerItemClickListe
ner(getActivity(), recyclerView, new MyRecyclerItemClickListener.
OnItemClickListener() {

  @Override
  public void onItemClick(View view, int position){
    // ...
  }
}
```

```
    @Override
    public void onItemLongClick(View view, int position){
      // ...
    }
}));


public class MyRecyclerItemClickListener implements RecyclerView.
OnItemTouchListener
{
  public static interface OnItemClickListener
  {
    public void onItemClick(View view, int position);
    public void onItemLongClick(View view, int position);
  }

  private OnItemClickListener mListener;
  private GestureDetector mGestureDetector;

  public MyRecyclerItemClickListener(Context context, final
RecyclerView recyclerView, OnItemClickListener listener)
  {
    mListener = listener;

    mGestureDetector = new GestureDetector(context, new
GestureDetector.SimpleOnGestureListener()
    {
      @Override
      public boolean onSingleTapUp(MotionEvent e)
      {
        return true;
      }

      @Override
      public void onLongPress(MotionEvent e)
      {
        View child = recyclerView.findChildViewUnder(e.getX(),
e.getY());

        if(child != null && mListener != null)
        {
          mListener.onItemLongClick(child, recyclerView.
getChildPosition(child));
        }
      }
```

```
        });
    }

    @Override
    public boolean onInterceptTouchEvent(RecyclerView view, MotionEvent
e)
    {
        View child = view.findChildViewUnder(e.getX(), e.getY());

        if(child != null && mListener != null && mGestureDetector.
onTouchEvent(e))
        {
            mListener.onItemClick(child, view.getChildPosition(child));
        }

        return false;
    }

    @Override
    public void onTouchEvent(RecyclerView view, MotionEvent motionEvent)
{
        //Empty
    }
}
@Override
public void onRequestDisallowInterceptTouchEvent(RecyclerView view){
    //Empty
}
```

The benefit of this approach is that we define what to do inside onClick in each activity or fragment. The logic of the click is not on the view, and once we build this component, we can reuse it in different apps.

The second approach is to set and manage the click inside ViewHolder. We will have a problem here if we want to reuse this ViewHolder in a different part of the app or in another app because the logic of the click is inside the view and we might want to have a different logic in different fragments or activities. However, this approach makes it easier to detect clicks on different components inside the same row. For instance, if we had a small icon to delete and another one to share the offer inside the row, this approach would make much more sense. This way, we can set the click on the job name in every row and a long click listener in the whole row:

```
public class MyViewHolder extends RecyclerView.ViewHolder implements
View.OnClickListener, View.OnLongClickListener{
```

```
    public TextView textViewName;
    public TextView textViewDescription;

    public  MyViewHolder(View v){
      super(v);
      textViewName = (TextView)v.findViewById(R.id.rowJobOfferTitle);
      textViewDescription = (TextView)v.findViewById(R.
id.rowJobOfferDesc);
      textViewName.setOnClickListener(this);
      v.setOnLongClickListener(this);
    }

    @Override
    public void onClick(View view) {
      switch (view.getId()){
        case R.id.rowJobOfferTitle :
        //Click
        break;
      }
    }

    @Override
    public boolean onLongClick(View view) {
      //Delete the element here
      return false;
    }
  }
}
```

You should be able to judge which implementation to use in every situation and argue in its favor. To be able to test this, we are going to delete an element after a long tap (we should have a confirmation dialog here to avoid deleting items by mistake but we will skip this part). The element will be deleted locally to display the remove animation. Note that we are not deleting this element from the source in Parse; all we need to do is to delete the element from the list and call notifyItemRemoved to trigger the notification. We will know which item is clicked on with the getPosition() method.

```
    @Override
    public boolean onLongClick(View view) {
      mOfferList.remove(getPosition());
      notifyItemRemoved(getPosition());
      return true;
    }
```

Summary

At the end of this chapter, you will know how to implement an Adapter, how to handle different types of items in lists, and how and why we apply the `ViewHolder` pattern. You first learned this along with the `ListView` class and manually implemented the recycling view techniques. As a result, you will be able to fully understand the features and how `RecyclerView` works in showing different ways to display the items and implement item click listeners.

In the next chapter, we will discover a new component introduced along with `RecyclerView` in Android 5.0— `CardView`. We will combine this with `RecyclerView` to have a flexible and professional-looking list of cards.

6
CardView and Material Design

In the first part of this chapter, we will improve our app significantly from a UI perspective and make it look professional by starting with a new widget: **CardView**. We will learn how to use design time attributes, which will improve our designing and development speed, and we will use a third party library to include custom fonts in an easy way in our entire app.

The second part will be focused on the design support library, adding material design concepts to our app, improving the tabs, and adding a parallax effect to the job offer view. During this, we will clarify what a toolbar, action bar, and app bar is, and how to implement up navigation from the app bar.

- CardView and UI tips:
    - CardView
    - Design time layout attributes
    - Custom fonts

- Design support library:
    - TabLayout
    - Toolbar, action bar, and app bar
    - CoordinatorLayout
    - Up navigation

CardView and UI design tips

At the moment, our application displays the job offers in a row with two text views; it displays the information needed and we can say that the app is fine as it is and it serves its purpose. However, we can still make a useful app and have a professional, good-looking interface at the same time, allowing us to be original and different from the competition. For instance, to show job offers, we can simulate a job board with adverts pinned on it. For this, we can use the CardView widget, which will give it depth and the appearance of a paper card. We will change the font of our app. A simple change such as this makes a big difference; when we change the default font to a custom font, the app from the users' eyes is a customized one, where the developer has taken care of the smallest details.

Introducing CardView

CardView was released with Android 5.0. It is a view with rounded corners and an elevation with shadows, thus providing a depth feel and simulating a card. Combining this with a recycler view, we get a great-looking list of items, with a behavior and look consistent with many apps. The following image is an example of a list with CardView and custom fonts:

While working with CardView, keep in mind that the rounded corners are implemented differently depending on the Android version. Padding is added to avoid clipping the child views in versions prior to Android 5.0, as also to achieve the shadow effect. In versions later than Android 5.0, shadows are displayed based on the property elevation from CardView, and any child intersecting with the rounded corners is clipped.

To start using CardView, we need to add it as a dependency from the project structure window or add the following line to the dependencies inside `build.gradle`:

```
dependencies {
  ...
  compile 'com.android.support:cardview-v7:21.0.+'
}
```

We can modify our `row_job_offer.xml` file with a base view as CardView with the content inside. This CardView will have some elevation and rounded corners. To set these attributes, we need to import CardView's own attributes by adding the following schema to the XML:

```
xmlns:card_view="http://schemas.android.com/apk/res-auto"
```

The following code will create the new layout:

```xml
<?xml version="1.0" encoding="utf-8"?>
<android.support.v7.widget.CardView
    xmlns:android="http://schemas.android.com/apk/res/android"
    xmlns:card_view="http://schemas.android.com/apk/res-auto"
    android:orientation="vertical" android:layout_width="match_parent"
    android:layout_height="170dp"
    android:layout_margin="10dp"
    card_view:cardElevation="4dp"
    card_view:cardCornerRadius="4dp"
    >
    <LinearLayout
        android:orientation="vertical"
        android:layout_width="wrap_content"
        android:padding="15dp"
        android:layout_height="wrap_content">
        <TextView
            android:id="@+id/rowJobOfferTitle"
            android:layout_width="fill_parent"
            android:layout_height="wrap_content"
            android:text="Title"
```

```
            android:textColor="#555"
            android:textSize="18sp"
            android:layout_marginBottom="20dp"
            />
        <TextView
            android:id="@+id/rowJobOfferDesc"
            android:layout_marginTop="5dp"
            android:layout_width="fill_parent"
            android:layout_height="wrap_content"
            android:text="Description"
            android:textColor="#999"
            android:textSize="16sp"
            />
    </LinearLayout>
</android.support.v7.widget.CardView>
```

We found a texture of a corkboard set it as a background, and on every card, we added a pin with an ImageView object at the top. The following is the achieved result:

The app looks much better than before; now, it's really a job board. By displaying the same information—the same two `TextView` with the title and job description—and simply changing the appearance, it evolved from a demo app to an app that could perfectly be launched in the Play Store.

We can continue improving this by changing the font, but before this, we will introduce the design time layout attributes, which will make the design of a view easier and quicker.

Design-time layout attributes

When working with design-time attributes, I always remember a funny story that took place in one of my first jobs. I had to display a list of contacts, so when I created the view of the contact, I used dummy data, which is used to assign some text while you create the view so that you can see the size, color, and general look in the design view.

The contact that I created was named *Paco el churrero*, or Frank the churros maker. Paco is a synonym for Francisco, and a churro—if you don't know—is a fried dough pastry. Anyway, this dummy data was changed to a proper contact name, and when the contact list was shown, these contacts were retrieved from a server. I can't remember whether I was in a hurry to release the app, I forgot to do it, or I simply missed it, but the app went live that way. I started to work on another component, and all was fine until one day, when there was a problem on the server side, and the server was sending empty contacts. The app was unable to override the dummy data with the contact name, and Paco el churrero was shown as a contact! Hopefully, the server was fixed before any user noticed.

After this, I created the view with dummy data, and once I was happy with the view, I removed the dummy data. However, with this approach, when I was asked for a UI change, I had to add the dummy data again.

With the release of Android Studio 0.2.11, the design-time layout attributes were born. These allow us to display text or any attribute in the design view that won't be there when you run the app; this data is only visible in the design view.

To use these, we need to add the namespace tools to our layout. The namespace is always defined in the root element of the view; you can find the line, `xmlns:android="http://schemas.android.com/apk/res/android`, and add the tools right after it. Use the following code:

```
<FrameLayout
xmlns:android="http://schemas.android.com/apk/res/android
xmlns:tools="http://schemas.android.com/tools"
```

To test this, we will add dummy text to the job offer and job description `TextView`:

```xml
<TextView
    android:id="@+id/rowJobOfferTitle"
    android:layout_width="fill_parent"
    android:layout_height="wrap_content"
    tools:text="Title of the job"
    android:textColor="#555"
    android:textSize="18sp"
    android:layout_marginBottom="20dp"
    />
<TextView
    android:id="@+id/rowJobOfferDesc"
    android:layout_marginTop="5dp"
    android:layout_width="fill_parent"
    android:layout_height="wrap_content"
    tools:text="Description of the job"
    android:textColor="#999"
    android:textSize="16sp"
    android:ellipsize="marquee"
    />
```

If you have problems rendering the design view, change the Android version or the theme, as in the following image. If the problem persists, ensure that you have the latest version of Android Studio and the latest Android API downloaded:

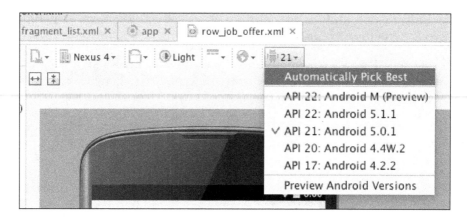

Once the view is rendered, we can see the job offer with the title and description from the design-time attributes.

You can use any attribute, text color, background color, and even image source, which is really useful when you create a view which contains an image that will be downloaded from the internet when the app is running, but you need a preview image to see how the view looks while creating it.

Working with custom fonts in Android

When working with customs fonts on Android, there is an amazing open source library — *Calligraphy* by Chris Jenkins — that allows us to set a default font for our whole app. This means that every widget with text, a Button, TextView, and EditText will show this font by default and we don't have to set the font individually for every single item in our app. Let's take a look at this in more detail and consider a few arguments in favor of Calligraphy.

If we want to apply a custom font, the first thing that we need to do is to place that font in the `assets` folder of our app. If we don't have this folder, we need to create it inside the `main` method, at the same level as `java` and `src`. Create a second folder, `fonts`, inside `assets` and place the font there. In our example, we will use the *Roboto* font; it can be obtained from Google fonts at `https://www.google.com/fonts#UsePlace:use/Collection:Roboto`. When the font is downloaded, the app structure should look similar to the following screenshot:

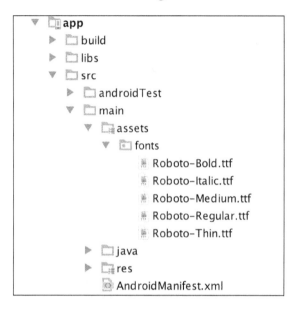

Once the font is in its place, we need to create a `Typeface` object from this font and set it to `myTextView`:

```
Typeface type = Typeface.createFromAsset(getAssets(),"fonts/Roboto-
Regular.ttf");
myTextView.setTypeface(type);
```

If we now wanted to apply the same font to all the components in our app, such as tabs, the title, and job offer cards, we would have to repeat the same code in different places around our app. Apart from this, we will also have performance issues. Creating a font from an asset requires access to the file; it is an expensive operation. If we changed the typeface for the job title and the job description inside the adapter, the view of our app wouldn't be fluent while scrolling anymore. This brings in extra considerations; for instance, we would have to load the typeface once in a static class and use it along with the app. Calligraphy handles all of this for us.

Another good reason to use calligraphy is that it allows us to set the font in the XML, so we can have different fonts in the same view and there is no need to set the typeface programmatically. We just need to add the `fontPath` attribute to the widget and optionally the `ignore` attribute to avoid warnings of Android Studio not detecting `fontPath`:

```
<TextView      android:text="@string/hello_world"      android:layout_
width="wrap_content"      android:layout_height="wrap_content"
fontPath="fonts/Roboto-Bold.ttf"
tools:ignore="MissingPrefix"/>
```

Now that we have explained the advantages of calligraphy, we can use it in our app. Add the following line to the dependencies in `build.gradle`:

```
compile 'uk.co.chrisjenx:calligraphy:2.1.0'
```

To apply a default font, add the following code to `Oncreate()` inside `MAApplication`:

```
CalligraphyConfig.initDefault(new CalligraphyConfig.Builder().
setDefaultFontPath("fonts/Roboto-Regular.ttf").setFontAttrId(R.attr.
fontPath).build());
```

And the following to any activity where we want to display the default font:

```
@Override protected void attachBaseContext(Context newBase) {super.att
achBaseContext(CalligraphyContextWrapper.wrap(newBase)); }
```

To finish, we can find a handwriting font that we like and set it to the card's title and description, which would look similar to the following output:

The design support library

The design support library introduces material design components in an official way and is compatible with all the versions of Android starting with Android 2.1. Material design is a new design language introduced with Android Lollipop. Before this library was released, we watched videos and considered examples of apps using these components, but there was no official way to use it. This established a baseline for the apps to follow; therefore, to master Android, we need to master material design. You can compile it using the following line:

```
compile 'com.android.support:design:22.2.0'
```

This library includes a visual component as the input text with floating text, floating action buttons, **TabLayout...**, and so on. However, material design is not only about visual components; it's about movement and transitions between its elements, and for this reason, **CoordinatorLayout** has been introduced.

Introducing TabLayout

The `TabLayout` design library allows us to have fixed or scrollable tabs with text, icons, or a customized view. As you would remember from the first instance of this in the book, customizing tabs wasn't very easy to do, and to change from scrolling to fixed tabs, we needed different implementations.

Now, we want to change the color and design of the tabs to be fixed; what we have to do first is go to `activity_main.xml` and add `TabLayout`, removing the previous `PagerTabStrip` tab. Our view will look as follows:

```xml
<?xml version="1.0" encoding="utf-8"?>
<LinearLayout
    android:layout_height="fill_parent"
    android:layout_width="fill_parent"
    android:orientation="vertical"
    xmlns:android="http://schemas.android.com/apk/res/android">
    <android.support.design.widget.TabLayout
        android:id="@+id/tab_layout"
        android:layout_width="match_parent"
        android:layout_height="50dp"/>
    <android.support.v4.view.ViewPager
        android:id="@+id/pager"
        android:layout_width="match_parent"
        android:layout_height="wrap_content">
    </android.support.v4.view.ViewPager>
</LinearLayout>
```

When we have this, we need to add tabs to the `Layout` tab. There are two ways to do this; one is to create tabs and add them manually as follows:

```
tabLayout.addTab(tabLayout.newTab().setText("Tab 1"));
```

The second way, which is how we will implement the tabs, is to set the view pager to `TabLayout`. Our `MainActivity.java` class should look as follows:

```java
public class MainActivity extends ActionBarActivity {

    @Override
    protected void onCreate(Bundle savedInstanceState) {
        super.onCreate(savedInstanceState);
        setContentView(R.layout.activity_main);

        MyPagerAdapter adapter = new MyPagerAdapter(getSupportFragmentMan
ager());
        ViewPager viewPager = (ViewPager) findViewById(R.id.pager);
        viewPager.setAdapter(adapter);

        TabLayout tabLayout = (TabLayout) findViewById(R.id.tab_layout);

        tabLayout.setupWithViewPager(viewPager);
    }

    @Override
    protected void attachBaseContext(Context newBase) {
        super.attachBaseContext(CalligraphyContextWrapper.wrap(newBase));
    }

}
```

If we don't specify any color, `TabLayout` uses the default color from the theme, and the position of the tabs is fixed. Our new tab bar will look as follows:

Toolbar, action bar, and app bar

Before proceeding to add motion and animations to our app, we need to clarify the concepts of toolbar, action bar, app bar, and `AppBarLayout` as these may cause a bit of confusion.

The action and app bar are the same component; "app bar" is just a new name that the action bar has acquired in material design. This is the opaque bar fixed at the top of our activity that usually shows the title of the app, navigation options, and displays different actions. The icon will or won't be displayed depending on the theme:

Since Android 3.0, the Holo theme or any of its descendants is used by default, and these show the action bar.

Let's move on to the next concept—toolbar. Introduced in API 21, Android Lollipop, it is a generalization of the action bar that doesn't need to be fixed at the top of the activity. We can specify whether a toolbar is acting as the activity action bar with the `setActionBar()` method. This means that a toolbar will or won't act as an action bar depending on what we want.

If we create a toolbar and set it as an action bar, we must use a theme with the `.NoActionBar` option to avoid having a duplicated action bar with the one that comes by default in a theme and the toolbar that we just converted into the action bar.

A new element called `AppBarLayout` has been introduced in the design support library. It is `LinearLayout`, intended to contain the toolbar to display animations based on scrolling events. We can specify the behavior while scrolling in the children with the `app:layout_scrollFlag`. `AppBarLayout` attribute. It is intended to be contained in `CoordinatorLayout`, and the component is introduced in the design support library as well, which we will describe in the following section.

Adding motion with CoordinatorLayout

The CoordinatorLayout allows us to add motion to our app, connecting touch events and gestures with views. We can coordinate a scroll movement with the collapsing animation of a view, for instance. These gestures or touch events are handled with the Coordinator.Behaviour class, and AppBarLayout already has this private class. If we want to use this motion with a custom view, we will have to create this behavior ourselves.

The CoordinatorLayout can be implemented in the top level of our app, so we can combine this with the application bar or any elements inside our activity or fragment. It also can be implemented as a container to interact with its child views.

Continuing with our app, we are going to show a full view of a job offer when we click on a card. This will be displayed in a new activity. This activity will contain a toolbar showing the title of the job offer and logo of the company. If the description is long, we will need to scroll down to read it; at this moment, we want to collapse the logo at the top as it is not relevant anymore. In the same way, while scrolling back up, we want it to expand again. To control the collapsing of the toolbar, we will need CollapsingToolbarLayout.

The description will be contained in NestedScrollView, which is a scroll view from the Android v4 support library. The reason for using NestedScrollView is that this class can propagate the scroll events to the toolbar, while ScrollView can't. Ensure that compile 'com.android.support:support-v4:22.2.0' is up to date.

We will see how to download images in the next chapter, so for now, we can just place an image from the drawable folder to implement the CoordinatorLayout functionality. In the next chapter, we will load the corresponding image for every company offering a job.

Our offer detail view, activity_offer_detail.xml, will look as follows:

```
<android.support.design.widget.CoordinatorLayout
xmlns:android="http://schemas.android.com/apk/res/android"
    xmlns:app="http://schemas.android.com/apk/res-auto"
    android:id="@+id/main_content"
    android:layout_width="match_parent"
```

```xml
        android:layout_height="match_parent">
    <android.support.design.widget.AppBarLayout
        android:id="@+id/appbar"
        android:layout_height="256dp"
        android:layout_width="match_parent">
        <android.support.design.widget.CollapsingToolbarLayout
            android:id="@+id/collapsingtoolbar"
            android:layout_width="match_parent"
            android:layout_height="match_parent"
            app:layout_scrollFlags="scroll|exitUntilCollapsed">
            <ImageView
                android:id="@+id/logo"
                android:layout_width="match_parent"
                android:layout_height="match_parent"
                android:scaleType="centerInside"
                android:src="@drawable/googlelogo"
                app:layout_collapseMode="parallax" />
            <android.support.v7.widget.Toolbar
                android:id="@+id/toolbar"
                android:layout_height="?attr/actionBarSize"
                android:layout_width="match_parent"
                app:layout_collapseMode="pin"/>
        </android.support.design.widget.CollapsingToolbarLayout>
    </android.support.design.widget.AppBarLayout>
    <android.support.v4.widget.NestedScrollView
        android:layout_width="fill_parent"
        android:layout_height="fill_parent"
        android:paddingLeft="20dp"
        android:paddingRight="20dp"
        app:layout_behavior="@string/appbar_scrolling_view_behavior">
            <TextView
                android:id="@+id/rowJobOfferDesc"
                android:layout_width="fill_parent"
                android:layout_height="fill_parent"
                android:text="Long scrollabe text"
                android:textColor="#999"
                android:textSize="18sp"
                />
    </android.support.v4.widget.NestedScrollView>
</android.support.design.widget.CoordinatorLayout>
```

As you can see, the `CollapsingToolbar` layout reacts to the scroll flag and tells its children how to react. The toolbar will be pinned at the top, always staying visible, `app:layout_collapseMode="pin"`. However, the logo disappears with a parallax effect, `app:layout_collapseMode="parallax"`. Don't forget to add to the `NestedScrollview` attribute, `app:layout_behavior="@string/appbar_scrolling_view_behavior"`, and clean the project to generate this string resource internally. If you have problems, you can set the string directly, `"android.support.design.widget.AppBarLayout$ScrollingViewBehavior"`, and this will help you identify the issue.

When we click on a job offer, we need to navigate to `OfferDetailActivity`, and we need to send the information of the offer. As you probably know from the beginner level, to send information between activities, we use intents. In these intents, we can put data or serialized objects. To be able to send an object of the `JobOffer` type, we have to create a `JobOffer` class that implements `Serializable`. Once we do this, we can detect the click on the element in `JobOffersAdapter`, as follows:

```java
public class MyViewHolder extends RecyclerView.ViewHolder implements
View.OnClickListener, View.OnLongClickListener{

    public TextView textViewName;
    public TextView textViewDescription;

    public  MyViewHolder(View v){
       super(v);
       textViewName = (TextView)v.findViewById(R.id.rowJobOfferTitle);
       textViewDescription = (TextView)v.findViewById(R.
id.rowJobOfferDesc);
       v.setOnClickListener(this);
       v.setOnLongClickListener(this);
    }

    @Override
    public void onClick(View view) {
       Intent intent = new Intent(view.getContext(), OfferDetailActivity.
class);
       JobOffer selectedJobOffer = mOfferList.get(getPosition());
       intent.putExtra("job_title", selectedJobOffer.getTitle());
       intent.putExtra("job_description",selectedJobOffer.
getDescription());
       view.getContext().startActivity(intent);
    }
```

Once we start the activity, we need to retrieve the title and set it to the toolbar. Add a long text to the `TextView` description inside `NestedScrollView` to test with dummy data first. We want to be able to scroll to test the animation:

```java
public class OfferDetailActivity extends AppCompatActivity {

    @Override
    protected void onCreate(Bundle savedInstanceState) {
        super.onCreate(savedInstanceState);
        setContentView(R.layout.activity_offer_detail);

        String job_title = getIntent().getStringExtra("job_title");

        CollapsingToolbarLayout collapsingToolbar =
        (CollapsingToolbarLayout) findViewById(R.id.collapsingtoolbar);
        collapsingToolbar.setTitle(job_title);

    }

}
```

Finally, ensure that your `styles.xml` file in the folder values uses a theme with no action bar by default:

```xml
<resources>

    <!-- Base application theme. -->
    <style name="AppTheme" parent="Theme.AppCompat.Light.NoActionBar">
        <!-- Customize your theme here. -->
    </style>

</resources>
```

We are now ready to test the behavior. Launch the app and scroll down. Take a look at how the image collapses and the toolbar is pinned at the top. It will look similar to the following screenshot:

We are missing an attribute to achieve a nice effect in the animation. Just collapsing the image doesn't collapse it enough; we need to make the image disappear in a smooth way, replaced by the background color of the toolbar.

Add the `contentScrim` attribute to `CollapsingToolbarLayout`, and this will fade in the image as it collapses using the primary color of the theme, which is the same as the one used by the toolbar at the moment:

```
<android.support.design.widget.CollapsingToolbarLayout
    android:id="@+id/collapsingtoolbar"
    android:layout_width="match_parent"
    android:layout_height="match_parent"
    app:layout_scrollFlags="scroll|exitUntilCollapsed"
    app:contentScrim="?attr/colorPrimary">
```

With this attribute, the app looks better when collapsed and expanded:

We just need to style the app a bit more by changing colors and adding padding to the image; we can change the colors of the theme in `styles.xml`:

```
<resources>
  <!-- Base application theme. -->
  <style name="AppTheme" parent="Theme.AppCompat.Light.NoActionBar">
    <item name="colorPrimary">#8bc34a</item>
    <item name="colorPrimaryDark">#33691e</item>
    <item name="colorAccent">#FF4081</item>
  </style>
</resources>
```

Resize `AppBarLayout` to `190dp` and add `50dp` `paddingLeft` and `paddingRight` to ImageView to achieve the following result:

Back navigation and up navigation

There are two ways of navigating to the previous screen. The one called back navigation is the navigation performed with the back button, which can be a hardware or software button depending on the device.

The **Up navigation** is a navigation method introduced with the action bar in Android 3.0; here, we can go back to the previous screen using an arrow pointing left, which is displayed in the action bar, as shown in the image to the right in the following screenshot:

On some occasions we need to override the functionality of the back navigation. For instance, if we have a custom `WebView` and we navigate through a browser, when we click on back, the back button will cause us to leave the activity by default; however, what we want is to go back in the history of the browser's usage:

```
@Override
public void onBackPressed() {
  if (mWebView.canGoBack()) {
    mWebView.goBack();
    return;
  }

  // Otherwise defer to system default behavior.
  super.onBackPressed();
}
```

Apart from this, the back navigation is implemented by default, unlike the Up navigation. To implement the Up navigation, we need an action bar (or a toolbar acting as an action bar), and we need to activate this navigation with the `setDisplayHomeAsUpEnabled(true)` method. Inside `onCreate` in our activity, we will add the following lines to set our toolbar as an action bar and to activate the Up navigation:

```
final Toolbar toolbar = (Toolbar) findViewById(R.id.toolbar);
setSupportActionBar(toolbar);
getSupportActionBar().setDisplayHomeAsUpEnabled(true);
```

This will display the back arrow at the top of our activity, as shown in the following screenshot. But at the moment, we won't have any functionality:

Once this is activated, we need to capture the click in the back arrow of the action bar. This will be detected as an action selection in the menu with the `android.R.id.home` ID; we just need to add the following code to our activity:

```
@Override
public boolean onOptionsItemSelected(MenuItem item) {
  switch (item.getItemId()) {
    case android.R.id.home:
    finish();
    return true;
  }
  return super.onOptionsItemSelected(item);
}
```

Summary

Our application has drastically changed in this chapter; we changed the job offer list completely and it now looks similar to a nice list of handwritten paper cards pinned onto a corkboard. At the same time, you learned concepts from material design and how to work with the application bar and the toolbar. There are more widgets in the design support library, such as InputText or FloatingButton, that are very easy to implement. It is as easy as adding a widget to a view, which is why we focused on the more difficult components such as CoordinatorLayout or CollapsingToolbarLayout.

In the next chapter, we will see how to download the logo of the company, advertise the job directly from a URL, talk about memory management, and take a look at how to make sure we don't have memory leaks in our app.

7
Image Handling and Memory Management

In this chapter, we will take a look at how to show images downloaded from a URL. We will discuss how to do this using the Android native SDK as well as the commonly used third-party libraries. We will consider key concepts and features such as download, compression, cache systems, and storage in memory or disk.

We will also discuss what a nine patch is and how to create it, and we will speak about the different size and density folder for drawables by introducing vector drawables.

The final section will be focused on memory management. Identifying memory leaks in our app is a critical task, which usually happens while working with images. We will take a look at the common mistakes that can lead to these leaks as well as general tips on how to prevent them.

- Displaying images from the network
    - The traditional way
    - Volley ImageDownloader
    - Picasso

- Images
    - Vector drawables
    - Animated vector drawables
    - Nine patch

- Memory management
  - ° Detecting and locating leaks
- Preventing leaks

Downloading images

Downloading an image and displaying it with the help of `ImageView` can be done in a single line. Since Android development started, this is something that every developer has done. Android is a technology that is more than five years old, so we can expect this technique to be quite advanced and to find-third party solutions that facilitate it. That said, this book wouldn't be called *Mastering Android* if it didn't explain the process of downloading an image and displaying it without any third-party library.

It is good to use the latest library in your apps, but it is better to understand the solution that you are implementing, and it is even better to be able to build this library yourself.

While working with images, we need to handle everything from network connection to the downloading of array bytes and their conversion to **Bitmap**. On some occasions, it makes sense to store the images on a disk so that the next time we open the app, these images will already be there.

Even if we are able to display an image, the matter doesn't finish here; we should be able to manage the downloading of images inside a list view. The downloading, storing, and displaying of systems need to be in sync for the app to work without glitches and have a fluent list that can scroll without problems. Keep in mind that when we scroll through a list, the views are recycled. This means that if we scroll fast, we might start the downloading of an image. By the time this download finishes, the view will not be visible on the screen anymore, or it will be recycled in another view.

The traditional way of downloading images

To display an image without using any third-party libraries (an image hosted on the Internet with a URL), we need to establish a connection using `HttpURLConnection`. We would need to open an input stream and consume the information, which can be transformed into a Bitmap image with the factory method, `BitmpapFactory.decodeStream(InputStream istream)`. We could convert it from an input stream to a file so that the image could be stored in the disk and accessed later. For the moment, let's try to download it first and convert it into a Bitmap image, which we will keep in the memory and show in `ImageView`.

We will show the logo of the company in `OfferDetailActivity` for every offer. Remember that in Parse, we created a database, and with it we created a field called `imageLink`. You just need to fill that field with the URL of the logo of that company.

company string	imageLink string	loca
SuitApps	http://suitapps.com/wp-content/uploads/201…	
Facebook	http://media.bestofmicro.com/R/0/464964/or…	
Recruiters LTD	https://media.licdn.com/mpr/mpr/shrinknp_8…	Rea
Recruiters LTD	https://media.licdn.com/mpr/mpr/shrinknp_8…	Rea
Recruiters LTD	https://media.licdn.com/mpr/mpr/shrinknp_8…	Rea
Yahoo	http://cdn3.wccftech.com/wp-content/upload…	Lon
Google	https://upload.wikimedia.org/wikipedia/com…	San

We need to have the image link in `OfferDetailActivity`; for this, we need to send an extra parameter in the intent in `JobOfferAdapter` for when we tap on a card. Use the following code:

```
@Override
public void onClick(View view) {
   Intent intent = new Intent(view.getContext(), OfferDetailActivity.
class);
   JobOffer offer = mOfferList.get(getPosition());
   intent.putExtra("job_title", offer.getTitle());
   intent.putExtra("job_description",offer.getDescription());
   intent.putExtra("job_image",offer.getImageLink());
   view.getContext().startActivity(intent);
}
```

The method in charge of the image download will be a static method that can be called from anywhere in the app. This method will be placed in the `ImageUtils` class inside a package called `utils`. We will first check whether the URL is correct, and after this, we will consume the content from `HttpURLConnection`, converting the input stream into a Bitmap image as we explained before:

```
public static Bitmap getImage(String urlString) {

   URL url = null;

   try {
     url = new URL(urlString);
   } catch (MalformedURLException e) {
```

```
      return null;
    }

    HttpURLConnection connection = null;
    try {
      connection = (HttpURLConnection) url.openConnection();
      connection.connect();
      int responseCode = connection.getResponseCode();
      if (responseCode == 200) {
        return BitmapFactory.decodeStream(connection.getInputStream());
      } else
        return null;
    } catch (Exception e) {
      return null;
    } finally {
      if (connection != null) {
        connection.disconnect();
      }
    }
  }
}
```

We will create a method called `displayImageFromUrl()` that receives `ImageView` and a string with the link to do all the work instead of having all this logic inside `onCreate`. In `onCreate`, we just need to retrieve the parameters and call the method:

```
String imageLink = getIntent().getStringExtra("job_image");
ImageView imageViewLogo = (ImageView) findViewById(R.id.logo);

displayImageFromUrl(imageViewLogo, imageLink);
```

At this stage, we can be tempted to call `ImageUtils.getImage(link)` and set Bitmap to `ImageView`. However, we are missing one thing; we can't just call the method that opens a network connection in the main activity thread. We need to do this in the background, or we would get an exception. An `AsyncTask` method is a nice solution to this problem:

```
String imageLink = getIntent().getStringExtra("job_image");
ImageView imageViewLogo = (ImageView) findViewById(R.id.logo);

displayImageFromUrl(imageViewLogo, imageLink);
```

```
public void displayImageFromUrl(ImageView imageView, String link){

    new AsyncTask<Object,Void,Bitmap>(){

      ImageView imageView;
      String link;

      @Override
      protected Bitmap doInBackground(Object... params) {
        imageView = (ImageView) params[0];
        link = (String) params[1];

        return ImageUtils.getImage(link);
      }

      @Override
      protected void onPostExecute(Bitmap bitmap) {
        super.onPostExecute(bitmap);
        imageView.setImageBitmap(bitmap);
      }

    }.execute(imageView, link);
}
```

Depending on the shape and background of the images used, it will look better with the ImageView attribute, scaleType, with the centerInside or centerCrop value. The CenterInside value will scale down the image to ensure that it fits in the recipient while keeping the proportions. The CenterCrop value will scale up the image until it fills the smallest side of the recipient. The rest of the image will go out of the bounds of ImageView.

At the beginning of the chapter, I mentioned that this could have been done just with a single line of code, but as you can see, doing it by ourselves takes much more than one line and involves different concepts such as background threading, HttpURLConnection, and so on. This is just the beginning; we implemented the simplest possible scenario. If we were setting the image in the same way in the rows of a list view, we would have problems. One of these problems would be firing infinite AsyncTask calls while scrolling. This could be controlled if we had a queue with a maximum number of AsyncTask and a cancellation mechanism to ignore or cancel the requests of the views that are not on the screen.

When we launch the `AsyncTask`, we have a reference to `ImageView`, and in `PostExecute`, we set `Bitmap` to it. This downloading operation can take some time so that `ImageView` can be recycled while scrolling. This means that we are downloading an image for `ImageView` that is recycled in a different position on the list to display a different element. For instance, if we had a list of contacts with their faces, we would see the faces of people with the wrong names. To solve this, what we can do is set the String with the image link to `ImageView` as a tag, `myImageView.setTag(link)`. If the view is recycled, it will have a different item with a new link; therefore, we can check in `onPostExecute`, just before displaying the image, whether the link that we have now is the same as the one in the `ImageView` tag.

These are two common problems and their respective solutions, but we haven't finished here. The most tedious thing, if we continue down this road, is to create a cache system. Depending on the application and on the situation, we might want to permanently store a downloaded image. For instance, if we were creating a music app with a list of your favorite albums, it would make sense to store the cover of an album in the disk. If you are going to see the list of favorites every time you open the app and we know that the cover is not going to change, why not store the image permanently so that the next time we open the app, it loads much quicker and doesn't consume any data? For the user, it would mean seeing the first screen loaded instantly all the time and be a huge improvement to the user's experience. To do this, we need to download the image on a file and have a third method to read the image from the file later, including the logic to check whether we already have this image downloaded or it's the first time that we have asked for it.

Another example can be a newsfeed reader app. We know that the images are going to change almost every day, so there is no point in keeping them on the disk. However, we might still want to keep them in memory while navigating through the app not to download them again in the same session while coming back to an activity from another. In this case, we need to keep an eye on the memory usage.

It's time to introduce some third-party libraries to help us with this topic. We can start with Volley, the same Volley that we implemented for network requests.

Downloading images with Volley

Volley offers two mechanisms to request images. The first mechanism, ImageRequest, is very similar to what we have just done with an AsyncTask using Volley's request queue and resizing the image on demand. This is the constructor for a request:

```
public ImageRequest(String url, Response.Listener<Bitmap> listener,
int maxWidth, int maxHeight, Config decodeConfig, Response.
ErrorListener errorListener) { … }
```

The maxWidth and maxHeight params will be used to resize the image; if we don't want to resize, we can set the value to 0. This is a method in our example used to fetch the image:

```
public void displayImageWithVolley(final ImageView imageView, String
url){

  ImageRequest request = new ImageRequest(url,
  new Response.Listener<Bitmap>() {
    @Override
    public void onResponse(Bitmap bitmap) {
      imageView.setImageBitmap(bitmap);
    }
  }, 0, 0, null,
  new Response.ErrorListener() {
    public void onErrorResponse(VolleyError error) {

    }
  });

  MAApplication.getInstance().getRequestQueue().add(request);
}
```

The second mechanism, the really interesting one, is ImageLoader. It handles multiple requests at the same time and is the mechanism to use in a list view for the reasons we explained in the previous section. We can create the cache mechanism that we want it to use—memory or disk.

It works using a special type of `ImageView`: `NetworkImageView`. When the
`ImageLoader` object is ready, we can simply download an image with one line using
`NetworkImageView`:

```
myNetworkImageView.setImage(urlString, imageloader);
```

It allows us to perform different operations such as setting a default image or setting
an image in case the request fails. Use the following code:

```
myNetworkImageView.sesetDefaultImageResId(R.id.default_image);
myNetworkImageView.setErroImageResId(R.id.image_not_found);
```

The complexity here, if there is any, comes when we implement `ImageLoader`.
First, we need to create it in the same way that we did with `RequestQueue` in the
`Application` class so that it can be accessed from anywhere in our app:

```
@Override
public void onCreate() {
  super.onCreate();

  sInstance = this;

  mRequestQueue = Volley.newRequestQueue(this);

  mImageLoader = new ImageLoader(mRequestQueue, new myImageCache());
```

The constructor needs a cache implementation. Google is an example of a memory-
based cache whose size is equal to three screens worth of images:

```
public class LruBitmapCache extends LruCache<String, Bitmap>
implements ImageCache {

  public LruBitmapCache(int maxSize) {
    super(maxSize);
  }

  public LruBitmapCache(Context ctx) {
    this(getCacheSize(ctx));
  }

  @Override
  protected int sizeOf(String key, Bitmap value) {
    return value.getRowBytes() * value.getHeight();
  }
```

```
  @Override
  public Bitmap getBitmap(String url) {
    return get(url);
  }

  @Override
  public void putBitmap(String url, Bitmap bitmap) {
    put(url, bitmap);
  }

  // Returns a cache size equal to approximately three screens worth
of images.
  public static int getCacheSize(Context ctx) {
    final DisplayMetrics displayMetrics = ctx.getResources().
    getDisplayMetrics();
    final int screenWidth = displayMetrics.widthPixels;
    final int screenHeight = displayMetrics.heightPixels;
    // 4 bytes per pixel
    final int screenBytes = screenWidth * screenHeight * 4;

    return screenBytes * 3;
  }
}
```

We can see that choosing between cache implementations is a manual process; we have to create the class with the implementation required and set it in the constructor of `ImageLoader`. That is why, the next library that we are going to see was a revolution when it came out.

Introducing Picasso

The same people that created `OkHttp` brought Picasso to the Android community. Picasso allows us to download and display an image in one line of code without creating an `ImageLoader` and with a cache implementation that automatically works using disk and memory. It includes image transformation, `ImageView` recycling, and request cancellations. All of this is free. It is unbelievable what the people at Square are bringing to the community.

If this is not enough, the debug mode will display indicators in the images, a small triangle in the corner with different colors to indicate when we download an image for the first time (which is when it comes from the network), when it comes from the memory cache, and when it comes from the disk cache:

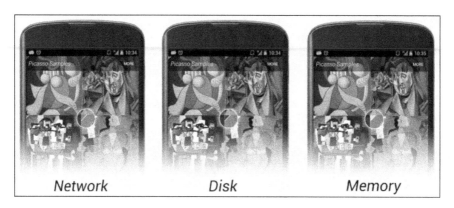

Mastering images

There are two concepts that we must cover in this book before finishing this chapter about images. As you know, the images can be placed in multiple folders depending on the density of the screen—from low-density `drawable-ldpi` to high-density `drawable-hdpi`, extra extra-extra high-density `drawable-xxxhdpi`, and possibly more in the future. When we do this, we need to consider whether we want top quality images in all screens or a light APK. Replicating images will increase the size of our installer. This problem will disappear with the following component introduced in Android 5.0.

Vector drawables

These drawables are based on vector graphics; vector graphics can be scaled up and scaled down without losing any quality. With this, we just need a single drawable, and it will have excellent quality no matter the screen we use for it, be it an Android watch or an Android TV.

Vector drawables are defined in the same way that we define a shape—in an XML file. This is a simple `vectordrawable.xml` file:

```
<vector xmlns:android="http://schemas.android.com/apk/
res/android" android:height="64dp" android:width="64dp"
android:viewportHeight="600" android:viewportWidth="600">
  <group>
    <path android:fillColor="@color/black_primary"
android:pathData="M12 36l17-12-17-12v24zm20-24v24h4V12h-4z" />
  </group>
</vector>
```

Note that the vector tag has a height and a width; if we set this drawable in `ImageView` and the size is smaller than the container, it will look pixelated.

You may be asking yourself, where do we get the `pathData` attribute from? You will probably have a `.svg` image, a format for scalable graphics. This image can be opened with a text editor, and you should be able to see something similar to the path data here:

```
<svg xmlns="http://www.w3.org/2000/svg" width="48" height="48"
viewBox="0 0 48 48">
  <path d="M12 36l17-12-17-12v24zm20-24v24h4V12h-4z"/>
</svg>
```

Google provides a pack of material design icons, and these icons come with an SVG version; with this, you can start adding infinite scalable images to your app. The path that we displayed is a media player icon from this pack of icons.

Vector drawable will be added to the design support libraries, so it will be possible to use it with the previous versions of Android, not only 5.0.

The next component might not be included in the design support library, so we will have to consider if we want to use it or not, depending on how extensive version 5.0 and above is. In any case, it's worth explaining it because sooner or later, it will be seen more due to its amazing results.

Animating with AnimatedVectorDrawable

As the name suggests, `AnimatedVectorDrawable` is a vector drawable with animations, and it is an important feature. These animations are not only rotation, scale, alpha, and so on, which are the ones we have seen previously in Android; these animations also allow us to transform the `pathData` attribute of the drawable. This means that we can have an image that changes shape or one that converts into another image.

This brings an infinite number of UI possibilities. For instance, we could have a play button converted into a semicircle that keeps spinning as a progress bar or a play button that transforms into a pause button.

We can define traditional animations, such a rotation, as follows:

```
<objectAnimator
  xmlns:android="http://schemas.android.com/apk/res/android"
  android:duration="6000"
  android:propertyName="rotation"
  android:valueFrom="0"
  android:valueTo="360" />
```

Here's how we can define the shape transformation from a triangle to a rectangle:

```
<set
  xmlns:android="http://schemas.android.com/apk/res/android">
  <objectAnimator
    android:duration="3000"
    android:propertyName="pathData"
    android:valueFrom="M300,70 l 0,-70 70,70 0,0    -70,70z"
      android:valueTo="M300,70 l 0,-70 70,0  0,140 -70,0 z"
    android:valueType="pathType"/>
</set>
```

To combine them together in an `AnimatedVectorDrawable` object, execute the following code:

```
<animated-vector
  xmlns:android="http://schemas.android.com/apk/res/android"
  android:drawable="@drawable/vectordrawable" >
  <target
    android:name="rotationGroup"
```

```
      android:animation="@anim/rotation" />
    <target
      android:name="v"
      android:animation="@anim/path_morph" />
  </animated-vector>
```

This is restricted to the paths with the same length and the same length of commands.

Working with the nine patch

Before explaining what a nine patch is, I will show you when it's needed. If we were doing a messaging application and we had to display what a user writes inside a chat bubble, we could think about creating `TextView` and setting an image of a message bubble as a background. If the message is very long, this is what happens without and with a nine patch background respectively.

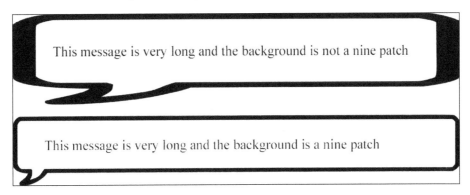

We can see that the first image is stretched, and it looks bad; however, we don't want to stretch the borders. What we want is to keep the borders the same but make the text area taller or wider depending on the message.

A nine patch image is an image that can be resized based on its content, but it involves leaving some areas without any stretching. It can be created from an image in a PNG file. Basically, it's the same PNG file with one pixel extra on every side and saved with the extension, `.9.png`. When we place this in the `drawable` folder, Android will know that in the extra pixel, there is information to know which areas to stretch and which ones to not.

If you look at the image, you will see that the extra pixel lines to the left and to the top are used to specify which content is scalable, and the lines to the bottom and to the right are used to specify which space can be filled. We want to fill the box completely, but we only want to scale a certain part to the left.

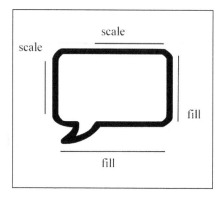

Android provides a tool to create these nine patch images, and you can find them in your SDK folder under `tools`. Just open `draw9patch` and drag an image into it.

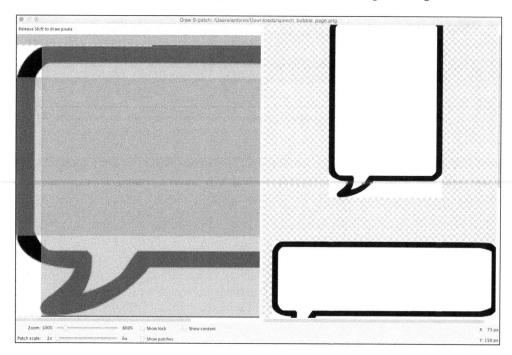

Memory management

Every Java developer has heard of the **garbage collector** (**GC**); this is a mechanism that automatically frees the resources in memory for us. On some occasions, we can prevent the garbage collector from freeing some resources; if the resources keep growing, we will inevitably see `OutOfMemoryError`.

If this happens, we need to locate the leak and then stop it. In this section, we will take a look at how to locate the source of the problem and a series of good practices to prevent this from happening.

This is not something to look into only when an error has occurred; our app might have leaks, not big enough to be detected with a quick test, that can lead to an error in a device with a smaller memory heap. Therefore, it's good to do a quick check on the memory levels before releasing an app.

Detecting and locating leaks

Android Studio provides a quick way to check the memory status. At the bottom window, you will find a tab called **Memory** next to `logcat` and the **ADB** logs.

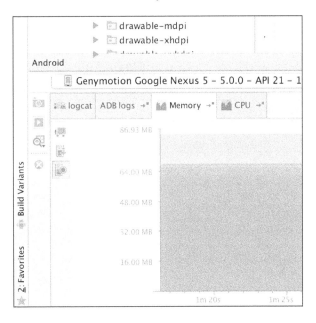

If you click on the small truck icon, which we call the garbage collector, you will see how the free memory increases.

Don't take this as a reference to the free memory because the heap is dynamic. This means that the heap can be 64 MB at first; we have 60 MB allocated and 4 MB free, but we allocate 10 MB more. The heap can grow higher, and we will end up having a 128 MB heap, with 70MB allocated and 58 MB free.

To detect a leak, we need to take the reference of the memory allocated. Click on the garbage collector constantly and navigate through the app, open and close activities, load images, scroll the lists, and perform these actions multiple times. If the allocated memory keeps growing and never goes down, it means that we are leaking memory and preventing some resources from being collected. We can roughly locate in which activity or fragment the leak is happening as we will see the increase always at the same point (assuming we don't have more than one leak).

To locate the source more precisely, we need to use **Android Device Monitor**:

Select your app process and click on **Update Heap**:

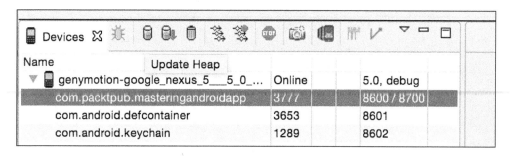

Once this is selected, we can see the allocations of the objects; this will be a good lead in case of bitmap or thread leaks:

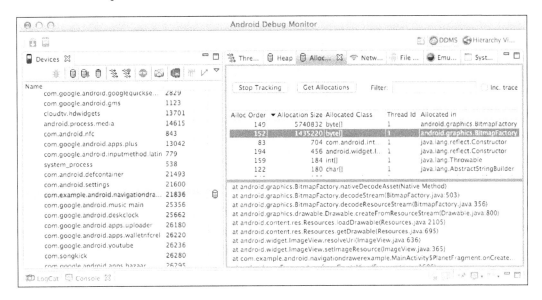

If we still have no clear idea of what is leaking the memory, we can click on the **Dum HPROF** file button and open this file with **MAT**, a memory analyzer tool from Eclipse. We will have to download Eclipse for this.

When we import the file, we can double-click in our process and click on **List Objects**, which will identify what is happening. For instance, we can see how many objects we have in an activity and how much heap is being used:

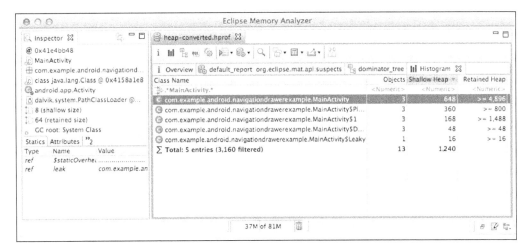

Preventing leaks

Better than fixing a memory leak is to not have it in the first place. If, during development, we keep in mind the most common causes of leaks, this will save us problems in the future.

Activity and context references

Activity references are one of the main causes of this problem. It's very common to send a reference of our activity to a download listener or to an event listener. If a reference to our activity is held in another object, this will prevent the garbage collector from freeing our activity. For instance, if we change the orientation, our activity will be created again by default, and the old activity with the old orientation will be destroyed.

Remember to unsubscribe from the listeners in the onDestroy method of our Activity and keep an eye on the objects where you send the Context; this is a strong reference to our Activity.

Using WeakReference

By default, when we create an object in Java, it is created with a hard reference. Objects different from null with hard references won't be garbage collected.

An object that contains only weak references will be garbage collected in the next cycle. The same object can have more than one reference; therefore, if we need to use an object temporarily, we can create a weak reference to it, and when the hard references are removed, it will be garbage collected.

This is a real-world example included in the Facebook SDK source code. They create a custom popup called **ToolTipPopup**, which looks similar to the following image:

This popup needs an anchor view, and this anchor view is referenced with a weak reference:

```
private final WeakReference<View> mAnchorViewRef;
```

The reason behind this is that by the time the popup is shown, we don't need the anchor view anymore. Once the popup is displayed, the anchor view can be set to null or made to disappear, and it won't affect us. Therefore, with a weak reference, if the original anchor view is destroyed and loses its hard references, it will also free the weak referenced object in the `ToolTipPopup` class.

Summary

In this chapter, you learned how to download an image without any help from third-party libraries in order to understand their usage. An overview of Volley and Picasso leaves us ready to implement any app with perfect handling. We also spent some time with images that are added into our app, such as vector drawables and nine patch images. To finish the chapter, we saw how to manage memory problems in our app, and more importantly, how to prevent them.

In the next chapter, we will create an SQLite database. We will export this database through a content provider and sync the UI data with this content provider through `CursorLoader`.

8

Databases and Loaders

In this chapter, we will create a SQLite database following a database contract and perform read/write operations using a database called **DAO** (**Data Access Object**). We will also explain the difference between a query and a raw query.

You will learn what a content provider is and how to create it, which will allow us to make this database accessible from `CursorLoader`. We will access the content provider through a content resolver and query different tables of the database at the same time, and you will learn how to use a join query in a content provider.

With `CursorLoader`, we'll be able to synchronize a list view with a database by creating a mechanism, where if we store or modify any data in the database, the changes will automatically be reflected in our view.

To finish, we will add the popular feature pull to refresh in order to update the content on demand. So, in this chapter, the following topics will be covered:

- Creating the database
    - Database Contract
    - Database Open Helper
    - Database Access Object

- Creating and accessing content providers
    - Content Provider
    - Content Resolver

- Syncing the database with UI
    - CursorLoader
    - RecyclerView and CursorAdapter

- Pull to refresh

Creating the database

To understand how databases work in Android, we will continue working on our example app, `MasteringAndroidApp`, creating a database to store the job offers that will be used to see the content in offline mode. This means that if we open the app once, the job offers will be kept in the device allowing us to see the information if opened without an Internet connection.

There are four mechanisms to persist data in Android:

- **Shared preferences**: These preferences are used to store basic information in a key-value structure

- **The internal storage**: This storage saves files that are private to your app

- **The external storage**: This storage saves files which can be shared with other apps

- **The SQLite database**: This database, based on the popular SQL, allows us to write and read information in a structured way

We can create simple structures, such as one-table databases, as well as complex structures with more than one table. We can combine the output of different tables to create complex queries.

We will create two tables so as to show how to create a join query using the content provider.

There will be a table for the companies, with the company ID, some information about them, name, website, extra information, and so on. A second table will include the job offers; this will also need to contain a column with the companies' IDs. If we want to have a tidy structure rather than having a big table with numerous fields, it's preferable to have the company information in the company table and the job offer in the job table, with just a reference to the company.

We won't alter the data structure in Parse for the sake of clarity and in order to focus on SQLite. Therefore, we will download the content and manually split the company and the job offer data, inserting them into separate tables.

Our company table will have the following structure:

RowId	Name	Image_link
0	Yahoo	....
1	Google	...

The `rowId` column is automatically added by Android, so we don't need to specify this column during the creation of the table.

The following table is the table of job offers:

RowId	Title	Description	Salary	Location	Type	Company_id
24	Senior Android..	2x developers	55.000	London,UK	permanent	1
25	Junior Android..	Dev with experience on..	20.000	London,UK	permanent	0

We will create a view as a result of joining these two tables; here, the join will be based on the `company_id`:

Title	Description	Salary	Location	Type	Company ID	Name	Image_link
Senior Android	2x developers..	55.000	London,UK	permanent	1	Google	…
Junior Android	Dev with experience on..	20.000	London,UK	permanent	0	Yahoo	…

This view will allow us to obtain all the data that we need in a single row.

The database contract

The database contract is a class where we define the name of our database and the name for all the tables and columns as constants.

It serves two purposes: firstly, it is a good way to have an idea of the structure of the database at first sight.

To create a database package and the `DatabaseContract.java` class, use the following code:

```
public class DatabaseContract {

    public static final String DB_NAME = "mastering_android_app.db";


    public abstract class JobOfferTable {
```

```java
    public static final String TABLE_NAME = "job_offer_table";

    public static final String TITLE = "title";
    public static final String DESC = "description";
    public static final String TYPE = "type";
    public static final String SALARY = "salary";
    public static final String LOCATION = "location";
    public static final String COMPANY_ID = "company_id";
    }


    public abstract class CompanyTable {

    public static final String TABLE_NAME = "company_table";

    public static final String NAME = "name";
    public static final String IMAGE_LINK = "image_link";
    }
    }
```

Secondly, using a reference to the constant avoids mistakes and allows us to make only one change in the value of a constant and propagate this over our entire app.

For instance, while creating this table in the database, we need to use the SQL sentence, CREATE TABLE "name"...; what we will do is use the name of the table from the contract with CREATE TABLE DatabaseContract.CompanyTable.TABLE_NAME....

The database contract is just the first step. It doesn't create a database; it's just a file that we use as a schema. To create the database, we need the help of SQLiteOpenHelper.

The database open helper

The open helper is a class that manages the creation and updating of the database. Updating is an important aspect that we need to keep in mind. Consider that we upload an app to Play Store, and after some time, we want to change the structure of the database. For instance, we want to add a column to a table without losing the data that the users of previous versions have stored in the old schema. Uploading a new version to Play Store, which deletes the previous information when the user updates our app, is not good for user experience at all.

To know when a database needs to be updated, we have a static integer with the database version that we have to manually increase if we alter the database, as follows:

```
/**
 * DATABASE VERSION
 */
private static final int DATABASE_VERSION = 1;
```

We need to create a `DatabaseOpenHelper` class that extends `SQLiteOpenHelper`. While extending this class, we are asked to implement two methods:

```
@Override
public void onCreate(SQLiteDatabase db) {
  //Create database here
}

@Override
public void onUpgrade(SQLiteDatabase db, int oldVersion, int
newVersion) {
  //Update database here
}
```

`SQLiteOpenHelper` will automatically call `onCreate` when we create an object of this class. However, it will only call this if the database is not created before and only once. In the same way, it will call `onUpgrade` when we increase the database version. That's why we need to send the params with the database name and the current version when we create an object of this class:

```
public DBOpenHelper(Context context){
    super(context, DatabaseContract.DB_NAME, null, DATABASE_VERSION);
}
```

Let's start with the creation of the database; the `onCreate` method needs to execute a SQL sentence on the database to create the table:

```
db.execSQL(CREATE_JOB_OFFER_TABLE);
db.execSQL(CREATE_COMPANY_TABLE);
```

We will define these sentences in static variables, as follows:

```
/**
 * SQL CREATE TABLE JOB OFFER sentence
 */
private static final String CREATE_JOB_OFFER_TABLE = "CREATE TABLE "
+ DatabaseContract.JobOfferTable.TABLE_NAME + " ("
+ DatabaseContract.JobOfferTable.TITLE + TEXT_TYPE + COMMA
+ DatabaseContract.JobOfferTable.DESC + TEXT_TYPE + COMMA
+ DatabaseContract.JobOfferTable.TYPE + TEXT_TYPE + COMMA
+ DatabaseContract.JobOfferTable.SALARY + TEXT_TYPE + COMMA
+ DatabaseContract.JobOfferTable.LOCATION + TEXT_TYPE + COMMA
+ DatabaseContract.JobOfferTable.COMPANY_ID + INTEGER_TYPE + " )";
```

By default, Android creates a `column_id` column, which is unique and autoincremental in every row; therefore, we don't need to create a column ID in the companies table.

As you can see, we also have the commas and types in the variable to avoid mistakes. It's very common to miss a comma or make a mistake when writing the sentence directly, and it's very time consuming to find the error:

```
/**
 * TABLE STRINGS
 */
private static final String TEXT_TYPE = " TEXT";
private static final String INTEGER_TYPE = " INTEGER";
private static final String COMMA = ", ";
```

We've seen how to create our tables, now we have to manage the update. In this case, we will simply drop the previous information and create the database again because there is no important information in the table. Once the app is opened after the update, it will download the job offers again and populate the new database:

```
@Override
public void onUpgrade(SQLiteDatabase db, int oldVersion, int
newVersion) {
  db.execSQL(DROP_JOB_OFFER_TABLE);
  db.execSQL(DROP_COMPANY_TABLE);
  onCreate(db);
}

/**
 * SQL DELETE TABLE SENTENCES
 */
```

```
public static final String DROP_JOB_OFFER_TABLE = "DROP TABLE IF
EXISTS "+ DatabaseContract.JobOfferTable.TABLE_NAME;
public static final String DROP_COMAPNY_TABLE = "DROP TABLE IF EXISTS
"+ DatabaseContract.CompanyTable.TABLE_NAME;
```

Our complete version of the class will appear as the following:

```
public class DBOpenHelper extends SQLiteOpenHelper {


    private static final int DATABASE_VERSION = 1;

    /**
     * TABLE STRINGS
     */
    private static final String TEXT_TYPE = " TEXT";
    private static final String INTEGER_TYPE = " INTEGER";
    private static final String COMMA = ", ";

    /**
     * SQL CREATE TABLE sentences
     */
    private static final String CREATE_JOB_OFFER_TABLE = "CREATE TABLE "
    + DatabaseContract.JobOfferTable.TABLE_NAME + " ("
    + DatabaseContract.JobOfferTable.TITLE + TEXT_TYPE + COMMA
    + DatabaseContract.JobOfferTable.DESC + TEXT_TYPE + COMMA
    + DatabaseContract.JobOfferTable.TYPE + TEXT_TYPE +

    COMMA        + DatabaseContract.JobOfferTable.SALARY + TEXT_TYPE +

    COMMA        + DatabaseContract.JobOfferTable.LOCATION + TEXT_TYPE +

    COMMA + DatabaseContract.JobOfferTable.COMPANY_ID +

    INTEGER_TYPE + " )";

    private static final String CREATE_COMPANY_TABLE = "CREATE TABLE "
    + DatabaseContract.CompanyTable.TABLE_NAME + " ("
    + DatabaseContract.CompanyTable.NAME + TEXT_TYPE + COMMA
    + DatabaseContract.CompanyTable.IMAGE_LINK + TEXT_TYPE +   " )";


    /**
     * SQL DELETE TABLE SENTENCES
     */
```

```
   public static final String DROP_JOB_OFFER_TABLE = "DROP TABLE IF
EXISTS "+ DatabaseContract.JobOfferTable.TABLE_NAME;
   public static final String DROP_COMPANY_TABLE = "DROP TABLE IF
EXISTS "+ DatabaseContract.CompanyTable.TABLE_NAME;

   public DBOpenHelper(Context context){
     super(context, DatabaseContract.DB_NAME, null, DATABASE_VERSION);
   }

   @Override
   public void onCreate(SQLiteDatabase db) {
     db.execSQL(CREATE_JOB_OFFER_TABLE);
     db.execSQL(CREATE_COMPANY_TABLE);
   }

   @Override
   public void onUpgrade(SQLiteDatabase db, int oldVersion, int
newVersion) {
     db.execSQL(DROP_COMPANY_TABLE);
     db.execSQL(DROP_JOB_OFFER_TABLE);
     onCreate(db);
   }
}
```

Database Access Object

Database Access Object, commonly known as **DAO**, is an object that manages all access to the database from the app. Conceptually, it's a class in the middle of the database and our app:

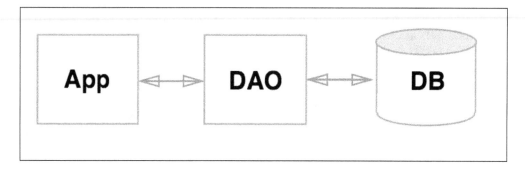

It's a pattern usually used in **J2EE (Java 2 Enterprise Edition**) on the server side. In this, the implementation of the database can be changed and added an extra layer of independency to, thus allowing the change in database implementation without changing any data in the app. Even if we do not change the implementation of the database in Android, (it will always be a SQLite database retrieved through `SQLiteOpenHelper`), it still makes sense to use this pattern. From a structural point of view, we will have all our database access operations in the same place. Also, using a DAO as a singleton with synchronized methods prevents issues such as trying to open the database from two different places at the same time, which can be locked if we are writing. Of course, the possibility to retrieve this singleton from anywhere in the app makes access to the database really easy as well.

In the next section, we'll take a look at how to create a content provider, which is an element that can replace our DAO object; however, content providers are tedious to implement if what we want is to just store and read data from the database. Let's continue with `MasteringAndroidApp`, creating a class called `MasteringAndroidDAO`, which will store the job offers and companies and show the information from the database in order to have an offline-working app.

This class will be a singleton with two public synchronized methods: one to store job offers (in the job offer table and the company table) and another to read them. Even if we split the information into two tables, while reading we will merge it again so that we can keep displaying the job offers with our current adapter without making major changes. Through this, you will learn how to join two tables in a query.

If a method is synchronized, we guarantee that it can't be executed from two places at the same time. Therefore, use the following code:

```
public class MasteringAndroidDAO {

    /**
     * Singleton pattern
     */
    private static MasteringAndroidDAO sInstane = null;

    /**
     * Get an instance of the Database Access Object
     *
     * @return instance
     */
```

```
    public static MasteringAndroidDAO getInstance(){
      if (sInstane == null){
        sInstane = new MasteringAndroidDAO();
      }
      return sInstane;
    }

    public synchronized boolean storeOffers(Context context,
  List<JobOffer> offers){
      //Store offers
    }


    public synchronized List<JobOffer> getOffersFromDB(Context context){
      //Get offers
    }


}
```

We will start with the `storeOffers()` method. The first thing that we need to do is open the database with `DatabaseOpenHelper`, and after this we need to start a transaction in the database. We will store a list of items, so it doesn't make sense to perform a transaction for each item. It's much more efficient if we open a transaction, perform all the insert operations that we need, and end the transaction after this, committing all the changes in a batch:

```
try {
  SQLiteDatabase db = newDBOpenHelper(context).getWritableDatabase();

  db.beginTransaction();
  //insert single job offer
  db.setTransactionSuccessful();
  db.endTransaction();
  db.close();
} catch ( Exception e){
  Log.d("MasteringAndroidDAO",e.toString());
  return false;
}
```

 Don't forget to close the database at the end with `db.close()`. Otherwise, it will remain open and consume resources, and we will get an exception if we try to open it again.

If we only had to insert data in a single table, we would only need to create a `ContentValue` object—a key-value object built based on the columns that we want to store—and call `db.insert(contentValue)`. However, our example is a little bit more complicated. To store a job offer, we need to know the company ID, and to obtain this ID, we need to ask our database if the company is already stored on it. If it's not, we need to store it and know which ID was assigned to it because, as we mentioned before, the ID is automatically generated and increased.

To find out if the company is already on the table, we need to perform a query searching all the rows to see if any row matches the name of the company that we are searching. There are two ways of performing a query: `query()` and `rawQuery()`.

Performing a query

A query needs the following parameters:

- `tableColumns`: This is the projection. We might want to return the columns that we want to return in the cursor in the whole table. In this case, it will be null, equivalent to `SELECT * FROM`. Alternatively, we might want to return just one column, `new String[]{"column_name"}`, or even a raw query. (here, `new String[]{SELECT ....}`).

- `whereClause`: Usually, the `"column_name > 5"` condition is used; however, in case the parameters are dynamic, we use `"column_name > ?"`. The question mark is used to specify the position of the parameters, which will come under the following `whereArgs` parameters.

- `whereArgs`: These are the parameters inside the `where` clause that will replace the question marks.

- `groupBy` (`having`, `orderby`, and `limit`): These are the rest of the params, which can be null if not used.

In our case, this is how we will ask if a company exists on the database. It will return a cursor with just one column, which is all we need to obtain the ID:

```
Cursor cursorCompany = db.query(DatabaseContract.CompanyTable.TABLE_
NAME,
    new String[]{"rowid"},
    DatabaseContract.CompanyTable.NAME +" LIKE ?",
    new String[]{offer.getCompany()},
    null,null,null);
```

The benefit of using `QueryBuilder` instead of `rawQuery` is the protection against SQL injections. At the same time, it's less prone to error. Performance-wise, it does not have any advantage as it creates `rawQuery` internally.

Using a raw query

A raw query is just a string with the SQL query. In our example, it would be as follows:

```
String queryString = "SELECT rowid FROM company_table WHERE name LIKE
'?'";
Cursor c = sqLiteDatabase.rawQuery(queryString, whereArgs);
```

In most cases, a raw query is more readable and needs less code to be implemented. In this case, a user with bad intentions could add more SQL code in the `whereArgs` variable to obtain more information, produce an error, or delete any data. It doesn't prevent SQL injection.

Introducing cursors

When we call `query()` or `rawQuery()`, the result is returned in a cursor. A cursor is a collection of rows with many methods to access and iterate it. It should be closed when no longer used.

The shortest way to iterate a cursor is to call `moveToNext()` in a loop, which is a method that returns false if there is no next:

```
Cursor c = query….
while (c.moveToNext()) {
  String currentName =
    c.getString(c.getColumnIndex("column_name"));
}
```

To read this information, we have different methods, such as `getString()`, which receives the index of the column of the value needed.

To know if a company is already on the table, we can execute a query, which will return a collection of rows with just one column of integers with the ID. If there is a result, the ID will be in the column with the `0` index:

```
public int findCompanyId(SQLiteDatabase db, JobOffer offer){
  Cursor cursorCompany = db.query(DatabaseContract.CompanyTable.TABLE_
NAME,
  new String[]{"rowid"},
  DatabaseContract.CompanyTable.NAME +" LIKE ?",
  new String[]{offer.getCompany()},
  null,null,null);

  int id = -1;
```

```
    if (cursorCompany.moveToNext()){
      id = cursorCompany.getInt(0);
    }
    return id;
}
```

Another option is to define the column with the name of the company as unique and to specify to ignore the conflicts using `insertWithOnConflict`. This way, if the company is already on the database or just inserted, it will return the ID:

```
db.insertWithOnConflict(DATABASE_TABLE, null, initialValues,
SQLiteDatabase.CONFLICT_IGNORE);
```

We can create a method for the query and get the ID from the cursor if there is a result. If not, the result will be -1. Before storing the job offer, we will check if the company exists. If not, we will store the company, and the ID will be returned during the insert:

```
public boolean storeOffers(Context context, List<JobOffer> offers){

  try {
    SQLiteDatabase db = new DBOpenHelper(context).
getWritableDatabase();

    db.beginTransaction();

    for (JobOffer offer : offers){

      ContentValues cv_company = new ContentValues();
      cv_company.put(DatabaseContract.CompanyTable.NAME, offer.
getCompany());
      cv_company.put(DatabaseContract.CompanyTable.IMAGE_LINK,offer.
getImageLink());

      int id = findCompanyId(db,offer);

      if (id < 0) {
         id = (int) db.insert(DatabaseContract.CompanyTable.TABLE_
NAME,null,cv_company);
      }

      ContentValues cv = new ContentValues();
      cv.put(DatabaseContract.JobOfferTable.TITLE,offer.getTitle());
      cv.put(DatabaseContract.JobOfferTable.DESC,offer.
getDescription());
```

```
        cv.put(DatabaseContract.JobOfferTable.TYPE, offer.getType());
        cv.put(DatabaseContract.JobOfferTable.DESC, offer.
getDescription());
        cv.put(DatabaseContract.JobOfferTable.SALARY,offer.getSalary());
        cv.put(DatabaseContract.JobOfferTable.LOCATION,offer.
getLocation());
        cv.put(DatabaseContract.JobOfferTable.COMPANY_ID,id);


        db.insert(DatabaseContract.JobOfferTable.TABLE_NAME,null,cv);
    }

    db.setTransactionSuccessful();
    db.endTransaction();

    db.close();

    } catch ( Exception e){
      Log.d("MasteringAndroidDAO", e.toString());
      return false;
    }

    return true;
}
```

Before testing this, it would be ideal to have the method to read from the database ready so that we can check that everything is stored correctly. The idea is to query both tables at the same time with a join query so as to get back a cursor with all the fields that we need.

In SQL, this would be a `SELECT * FROM job_offer_table JOIN company_table ON job_offer_table.company_id = company_table.rowid` ... query.

We need to do this in a query using the name of the tables from the database contract. This is how it will look:

```
public List<JobOffer> getOffersFromDB(Context context){

    SQLiteDatabase db = new DBOpenHelper(context).getWritableDatabase();

    String join = DatabaseContract.JobOfferTable.TABLE_NAME + " JOIN " +
    DatabaseContract.CompanyTable.TABLE_NAME + " ON " +
```

```
  DatabaseContract.JobOfferTable.TABLE_NAME+"."+DatabaseContract.
JobOfferTable.COMPANY_ID
    +" = " + DatabaseContract.CompanyTable.TABLE_NAME+".rowid";

    Cursor cursor = db.query(join,null,null,null,null,null,null);

    List<JobOffer> jobOfferList = new ArrayList<>();

    while (cursor.moveToNext()) {
      //Create job offer from cursor and add it
      //to the list
    }

    cursor.close();
    db.close();

    return jobOfferList;
  }
```

The next step is to create a job offer object from a cursor row and add it to the job offer list:

```
while (cursor.moveToNext()) {

    JobOffer offer = new JobOffer();
    offer.setTitle(cursor.getString(cursor.
getColumnIndex(DatabaseContract.JobOfferTable.TABLE_NAME)));
    offer.setDescription(cursor.getString(cursor.
getColumnIndex(DatabaseContract.JobOfferTable.DESC)));
    offer.setType(cursor.getString(cursor.
getColumnIndex(DatabaseContract.JobOfferTable.TYPE)));
    offer.setSalary(cursor.getString(cursor.
getColumnIndex(DatabaseContract.JobOfferTable.SALARY)));
    offer.setLocation(cursor.getString(cursor.
getColumnIndex(DatabaseContract.JobOfferTable.LOCATION)));
    offer.setCompany(cursor.getString(cursor.
getColumnIndex(DatabaseContract.CompanyTable.NAME)));
    offer.setImageLink(cursor.getString(cursor.
getColumnIndex(DatabaseContract.CompanyTable.IMAGE_LINK)));

    jobOfferList.add(offer);
}
```

For this example, we will clear the database when we add new data. For this, we will create a method in `MasteringAndroidDAO`:

```
/**
* Remove all offers and companies
*/
public void clearDB(Context context)
{
   SQLiteDatabase db = new DBOpenHelper(context).getWritableDatabase();
   // db.delete(String tableName, String whereClause, String[]
whereArgs);
   // If whereClause is null, it will delete all rows.
   db.delete(DatabaseContract.JobOfferTable.TABLE_NAME, null, null);
   db.delete(DatabaseContract.CompanyTable.TABLE_NAME, null, null);
}
```

Once the database access object has all the methods that we will need, we have to move to `ListFragment` and implement the logic. The ideal flow would be to first show the data from the database and fire the download to get the new job offers. In the background, the offers will be updated and the list will be refreshed when the update is finished. We will do this with the content provider and a cursor loader that connects the database automatically with the list view. For this example, to test the DAO, we will simply show the data from the database if there is no internet connection or get a new list of job offers. When the new list is downloaded, we will clear the database and store the new offers.

If we wanted to build a system that keeps a history of the job offers instead of clearing the database, what we would have to do is check if there are any new offers coming from the server that are not stored already in the database and save only the new offers. This can be easily done by creating a new column with the ID from Parse so that we can compare job offers with a unique identifier.

To check if there is an Internet connection, we will ask the connectivity manager using the following code:

```
public boolean isOnline() {
   ConnectivityManager cm =
   (ConnectivityManager) getActivity().getSystemService(Context.
CONNECTIVITY_SERVICE);
   NetworkInfo netInfo = cm.getActiveNetworkInfo();
   return netInfo != null && netInfo.isConnectedOrConnecting();
}
```

In the `onCreateView` method, we need to ask whether or not there is a connection. If there is a connection, we can download a new list of offers, which will be shown and stored in the database, thus clearing the previous offers:

```
@Override
public View onCreateView(LayoutInflater inflater, ViewGroup container,
Bundle savedInstanceState) {
  // Inflate the layout for this fragment
  View view = inflater.inflate(R.layout.fragment_list, container,
false);

  mRecyclerView = (RecyclerView) view.findViewById(R.id.my_recycler_
view);

  // use this setting to improve performance if you know that changes
  // in content do not change the layout size of the RecyclerView
  mRecyclerView.setHasFixedSize(true);

  // use a linear layout manager
  mRecyclerView.setLayoutManager(new LinearLayoutManager(getActivi
ty()));

  //Retrieve the list of offers

  if (isOnline()){
    retrieveJobOffers();
  } else {
    showOffersFromDB();
  }

  return view;
}


public void retrieveJobOffers(){
  ParseQuery<JobOffer> query = ParseQuery.getQuery("JobOffer");
  query.findInBackground(new FindCallback<JobOffer>() {

    @Override
    public void done(List<JobOffer> jobOffersList, ParseException e) {
      MasteringAndroidDAO.getInstance().clearDB(getActivity());
```

```
        MasteringAndroidDAO.getInstance().storeOffers(getActivity(),
    jobOffersList);
        mListItems = MasteringAndroidDAO.getInstance().
    getOffersFromDB(getActivity());
        JobOffersAdapter adapter = new JobOffersAdapter(mListItems);
        mRecyclerView.setAdapter(adapter);
      }

    });
  }

  public void showOffersFromDB(){
    mListItems = MasteringAndroidDAO.getInstance().
  getOffersFromDB(getActivity());
    JobOffersAdapter adapter = new JobOffersAdapter(mListItems);
    mRecyclerView.setAdapter(adapter);
  }
```

At the moment, we will create the adapter with a new list of elements. If we want to update the list view on the screen with new job offers and we use this method, it will restart the adapter, which will make the list empty for a second and move the scrolling position to the top. We shouldn't create an adapter to refresh the list; the existing adapter should update the list of elements.

To do this, we would have to create an `updateElements()` method in the adapter that replaces the current list of offers and calls `notifiyDataSetChanged()`, causing the adapter to refresh all the elements. If we know exactly how many elements we have updated, we can use `notifyItemInserted()` or `notifyRangeItemInserted()` to update and animate only the new elements added, which works more efficiently than `notifyDataSetChanged()`.

There is no need to do this synchronization of the view with the data manually. Android provides us with `CursorLoader`, a mechanism that connects the list view with the database directly. So, all we need to do is store the new offers in the database, and the list view will automatically reflect our changes. However, all of this automation comes at a cost; it needs a content provider to work.

Content providers

A content provider is very similar to the concept of a DAO; it is an interface between the data and the app that allows different apps to exchange information. We can decide whether we want it to be public or not, whether we want other apps to be able to get data from it, and whether it will only be used internally in our app. The data can be stored in a database such as the one we are about to create. It can be stored in files; for instance, if we want access to videos or pictures from the gallery, we'll use an Android built-in media content provider. Alternatively, it can be obtained from the network:

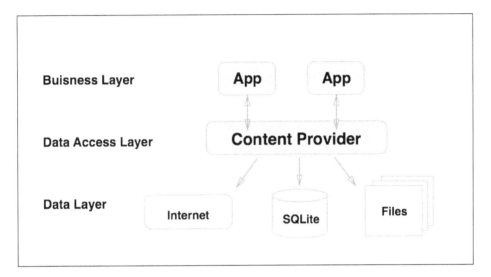

A content provider must be declared in the manifest as it is a component of our app and also specify whether or not it will be accessible to other apps, which is controlled by the attribute exported. Let's start by creating our own content provider.

To create a content provider, create a `MAAProvider` class and extend
`ContentProvider`. We will be asked to implement the following methods:

```java
public class MAAProvider extends ContentProvider {

    @Override
    public boolean onCreate() {
        return false;
    }

    @Override
    public Cursor query(Uri uri, String[] projection, String selection,
    String[] selectionArgs, String sortOrder) {
        return null;
    }

    @Override
    public Uri insert(Uri uri, ContentValues values) {
        return null;
    }

    @Override
    public int delete(Uri uri, String selection, String[] selectionArgs)
    {
        return 0;
    }

    @Override
    public int update(Uri uri, ContentValues values, String selection,
    String[] selectionArgs) {
        return 0;
    }


    @Override
    public String getType(Uri uri) {
        return null;
    }
}
```

The `OnCreate` method will be called when the provider is started; it will initialize all the elements required for the provider to work. The provider will start at the same time as the application. The system knows which provider to start because it's defined in the manifest. The next four methods are the methods to access and manage the data. The final method returns the MIME type of the object.

As we mentioned before, there are different content providers in the phone that we can use; for example, we can access the SMS, contacts, or media items from the gallery using a content provider. So, there must be a way to identify and access each one of them. This is done with a **URI (Uniform Resource Identifier)**, which is a string similar to a URL that we use to go to a website in the browser.

A URI is composed of a prefix, `"content://"`, followed by a string identifier, called authority. It is usually the name of the class plus the package `"com.packtpub.masteringandoridapp.MAAProvider"` followed by a slash and the name of the table, for instance `"/company_table"`. It is also followed optionally by a slash and the number of the row inside the table `"/2"`.

Therefore, the complete URI for the company table will be `"content://com.packtub.masteringandroidapp.MAAProvider/company_table`.

The complete URI for the company with ID number 2 will be `"content://com.packtub.masteringandroidapp.MAAProvider/company_table/2"`. This URI would be represented as `company_table/#` in a general way, where # will be replaced by an integer.

Given that we have two different tables and a third one, which is the result of the join (which can be accessed to get all the elements on the table or to get a single row), we have six possible URIs:

- `content://com.packtub.masteringandroidapp.MAAProvider/company_table`
- `content://com.packtub.masteringandroidapp.MAAProvider/company_job_offer`
- `content://com.packtub.masteringandroidapp.MAAProvider/offer_join_company`
- `content://com.packtub.masteringandroidapp.MAAProvider/company_table/#`
- `content://com.packtub.masteringandroidapp.MAAProvider/company_job_offer/#`
- `content://com.packtub.masteringandroidapp.MAAProvider/offer_join_company/#`

We have only one content provider; in theory, this provider can implement the query, insert, update, delete, and getType methods for all six URIs, each with six different implementations. Therefore, when we perform myMAAProvider. insert(URI ...), we will need to have an if statement to see which of the tables needs an insert and choose the right implementations. It would be something similar to this:

```
@Override
public Uri insert(Uri uri, ContentValues values) {
    if (uri.equals("content://com.packtub.masteringandroidapp.
MAAProvider/company_table")){
        //Do an insert in company_table
    } else if (uri.equals("content://com.packtub.masteringandroidapp.
MAAProvider/offer_table")){
    //Do an insert in offer table
    } else if ... {
        .

        .

        .

    }
    }
```

As you can see by comparing the strings, this doesn't seem right, and if we add a URI with an integer at the end, we would need some mechanism to verify that "company_table/2" corresponds to the general URI, "company_table/#". This is why we have UriMatcher. UriMatcher, which will contain a list of the possible URL's associated with an integer. So, when it receives a URI, it will tell us which integer to use while using string patterns.

After creating UriMatcher and defining all the possible cases, we can just add the possible cases to UriMatcher and call UriMatcher.match(Uri uri), which will return an integer with the case. All we need to do is a switch to check which case we are in:

```
public class MAAProvider extends ContentProvider {

    public final String authority = "com.packtpub.masteringandroidapp.
MAAProvider";

    private UriMatcher mUriMatcher;

    private static final int COMPANY_TABLE = 0;
    private static final int COMPANY_TABLE_ROW = 1;
    private static final int OFFER_TABLE = 2;
```

```
private static final int OFFER_TABLE_ROW = 3;
private static final int JOIN_TABLE = 4;
private static final int JOIN_TABLE_ROW = 5;

@Override
public boolean onCreate() {
  mUriMatcher = new UriMatcher(UriMatcher.NO_MATCH);
  mUriMatcher.addURI(authority,DatabaseContract.CompanyTable.TABLE_
NAME,COMPANY_TABLE);
  mUriMatcher.addURI(authority,DatabaseContract.CompanyTable.TABLE_
NAME+"/#",COMPANY_TABLE_ROW);
  mUriMatcher.addURI(authority,DatabaseContract.JobOfferTable.TABLE_
NAME,OFFER_TABLE);
  mUriMatcher.addURI(authority,DatabaseContract.JobOfferTable.TABLE_
NAME+"/#",OFFER_TABLE_ROW);
  mUriMatcher.addURI(authority,DatabaseContract.OFFER_JOIN_
COMPANY,JOIN_TABLE);
  mUriMatcher.addURI(authority,DatabaseContract.OFFER_JOIN_
COMPANY+"/#",JOIN_TABLE_ROW);

  mDB = new DBOpenHelper(getContext()).getWritableDatabase();

  return true;
}


@Override
public Cursor query(Uri uri, String[] projection, String selection,
String[] selectionArgs, String sortOrder) {
  switch (mUriMatcher.match(uri)){
    case COMPANY_TABLE:
    //Query company table
    break;
    case COMPANY_TABLE_ROW:
    //Query company table by id
    break;
    .
    .
```

We can start implementing the query method to get a list of offers merged with companies and set it to the adapter to check that everything is working well so far. We need to have the following variable with the database:

```
private SQLiteDatabase mDB;
```

This will be assigned in `onCreate` as follows:

```
mDB = new DBOpenHelper(getContext()).getWritableDatabase();
```

Also, in the query method, we need to create a query for the six possibilities, as follows:

```
@Override
public Cursor query(Uri uri, String[] projection, String selection,
String[] selectionArgs, String sortOrder) {
  switch (mUriMatcher.match(uri)){
    case COMPANY_TABLE:
    return mDB.query(DatabaseContract.CompanyTable.TABLE_NAME, project
ion,selection,selectionArgs,null,null,sortOrder);
    case COMPANY_TABLE_ROW:
    selection = "rowid LIKE "+uri.getLastPathSegment();
    return mDB.query(DatabaseContract.CompanyTable.TABLE_NAME, project
ion,selection,selectionArgs,null,null,sortOrder);
    case OFFER_TABLE:
    return mDB.query(DatabaseContract.JobOfferTable.TABLE_NAME, projec
tion,selection,selectionArgs,null,null,sortOrder);
    case OFFER_TABLE_ROW:
    selection = "rowid LIKE "+uri.getLastPathSegment();
    return mDB.query(DatabaseContract.JobOfferTable.TABLE_NAME, projec
tion,selection,selectionArgs,null,null,sortOrder);
    case JOIN_TABLE:
    return mDB.query(DBOpenHelper.OFFER_JOIN_COMPANY, projection,selec
tion,selectionArgs,null,null,sortOrder);
    case JOIN_TABLE_ROW:
    selection = "rowid LIKE "+uri.getLastPathSegment();
    return mDB.query(DBOpenHelper.OFFER_JOIN_COMPANY, projection,selec
tion,selectionArgs,null,null,sortOrder);
  }
  return null;
}
```

We need to do this with the `DBOpenHelper.OFFER_JOIN_COMPANY` variable defined as follows:

```
public static final String OFFER_JOIN_COMPANY = DatabaseContract.
JobOfferTable.TABLE_NAME + " JOIN " +
DatabaseContract.CompanyTable.TABLE_NAME + " ON " +
DatabaseContract.JobOfferTable.TABLE_NAME+"."+DatabaseContract.
JobOfferTable.COMPANY_ID
+" = " + DatabaseContract.CompanyTable.TABLE_NAME+".rowid";Content
Resolver
```

To access a content provider, we will use `ContentResolver`. It is a general instance that provides access to all the content providers available as well as to CRUD operations (create, read, update, and delete):

```
ContentResolver cr = getContentResolver();
```

To use the content resolver, we need a URI for the content provider. We can create it from a string variable right before making the call:

```
Uri uriPath = Uri.parse("content://"+MAAProvider.authority + "/" +
DatabaseContract.OFFER_JOIN_COMPANY);
Cursor cursor = cr.query(uriPath, null, null, null, null);
```

Alternatively, we can define a list of URI in the provider as a static variable access to them.

If we try to run this code now, we would get the error, '*failed to find provider info for com.packtub.masteringandroidapp.MAAProvider*'. This means that the system can't find the provider because we haven't added it to the manifest yet.

To add a provider, we need to add the `<provider>` element within the `<application>` tag; it needs the path and name of our provider and the authority. In our case, both are the same:

```
        .
        .
        .
    <activity
        android:name=".OfferDetailActivity"
        android:label="@string/title_activity_offer_detail" >
    </activity>
    <provider android:name="com.packtpub.masteringandroidapp.
MAAProvider"
        android:authorities="com.packtpub.masteringandroidapp.
MAAProvider">
    </provider>
</application>
```

Even if we display the data with `CursorLoader` and do not use the list of offers content, it wouldn't be a bad idea to create a temporary method that displays the list of offers from the content provider. It helps ensure that the content provider is accessible and returns the expected data before going further down in the CursorLoader road:

```
public void showOffersFromContentProvider(){
    ContentResolver cr = getActivity().getContentResolver();
```

```
    Uri uriPath = Uri.parse("content://"+MAAProvider.authority + "/" +
DatabaseContract.OFFER_JOIN_COMPANY);
    Cursor cursor = cr.query(uriPath, null, null, null, null);

    List<JobOffer> jobOfferList = new ArrayList<>();
    while (cursor.moveToNext()) {

        JobOffer offer = new JobOffer();
        offer.setTitle(cursor.getString(cursor.
getColumnIndex(DatabaseContract.JobOfferTable.TITLE)));
        offer.setDescription(cursor.getString(cursor.
getColumnIndex(DatabaseContract.JobOfferTable.DESC)));
        offer.setType(cursor.getString(cursor.
getColumnIndex(DatabaseContract.JobOfferTable.TYPE)));
        offer.setSalary(cursor.getString(cursor.
getColumnIndex(DatabaseContract.JobOfferTable.SALARY)));
        offer.setLocation(cursor.getString(cursor.
getColumnIndex(DatabaseContract.JobOfferTable.LOCATION)));
        offer.setCompany(cursor.getString(cursor.
getColumnIndex(DatabaseContract.CompanyTable.NAME)));
        offer.setImageLink(cursor.getString(cursor.
getColumnIndex(DatabaseContract.CompanyTable.IMAGE_LINK)));

        jobOfferList.add(offer);
    }
    JobOffersAdapter adapter = new JobOffersAdapter(jobOfferList);
    mRecyclerView.setAdapter(adapter);
}
```

By replacing the call to showOffersFromDB() with
showOffersFromContentProvider(), we should see exactly the same information
in the same order:

```
if (isOnline()){
    retrieveJobOffers();
} else {
    showOffersFromContentProvider();
}
```

The CursorLoader object can be easily implemented once the provider is created. At
this stage, we can say that most of the job is done.

Sync database with UI

When we use CursorLoader with a content provider, the data returned in the cursor is directly connected with the data in the database in such a way that one change in the database is reflected instantly in the UI. When we have this system working, all we need to worry about is storing the data in the database and updating the data. When we have this system ready, we will discuss how to implement the popular pull to refresh system to update the job offers at the time the user wants. The goal is to add a new job offer in Parse, pull the list to refresh, and see the new element come instantly, all handled in the background through the content provider.

Implementing CursorLoader

To complete this goal, the next step is to create CursorLoader. We talked about loaders previously in the book; as we mentioned, they are a mechanism to load data in the background. This one specifically will return the data in a cursor and load it from a content provider. It will also refresh the data when any change in the source is detected.

To start using CursorLoader, our Activity or Fragment — FragmentList in our case — needs to implement LoaderManager.LoaderCallback<Callback>. This interface will ask us to implement the following methods:

```
public class ListFragment extends android.support.v4.app.Fragment
implements LoaderManager.LoaderCallbacks<Cursor>

@Override
public Loader<Cursor> onCreateLoader(int id, Bundle args) {
  return null;
}

@Override
public void onLoadFinished(Loader<Cursor> loader, Cursor data) {

}

@Override
public void onLoaderReset(Loader<Cursor> loader) {

}
```

Let's start with the first method—onCreateLoader. This method receives an integer ID as a parameter, which will be the ID of our loader. We can have more than one loader working in the same activity, so we will assign an ID to them in order to be able to identify them. Our loader will be defined as:

```
public static final int MAA_LOADER = 1;
```

The OnCreateLoader method will be executed when we tell LoaderManager to initialize our loader. This can be done in onCreateView():

```
getLoaderManager().initLoader(MAA_LOADER, null, this);
```

This method has to create all the different loaders that can be initialized (they can be different types of loaders); in our case, we will only have one, which will be CursorLoader. It will query the table and join the offers' table with the companies' table as a result. The string with the content URI has been defined previously in MAAProvider:

```
public static final String JOIN_TABLE_URI =  "content://" +
MAAProvider.authority + "/" + DatabaseContract.OFFER_JOIN_COMPANY;
@Override
public Loader<Cursor> onCreateLoader(int loaderID, Bundle bundle)
{
  switch (loaderID) {
    case MAA_LOADER:
    return new CursorLoader(
    getActivity(),    // Parent activity context
    Uri.parse(MAAProvider.JOIN_TABLE_URI),
    // Table to query
    null,              // Projection to return
    null,              // No selection clause
    null,              // No selection arguments
    null               // Default sort order
    );
    default:
    //Invalid ID
    return null;
  }
}
```

When we tell the loader manager to initialize our loader, it automatically creates it and starts running the query to the database; asynchronously, it will call the second method implemented, which is onLoadFinished. In this method, as an example, we can retrieve the cursor and display the data, just as we did before while getting the cursor from the content resolver. By moving the code that we use to create the job offer from the course to a static method in the JobOffer class, our onLoadFinished method will look similar to the following:

```
@Override
public void onLoadFinished(Loader<Cursor> loader, Cursor cursor) {

    List<JobOffer> jobOfferList = new ArrayList<>();

    while (cursor.moveToNext()) {
      jobOfferList.add(JobOffer.createJobOfferfromCursor(cursor));
    }

    JobOffersAdapter adapter = new JobOffersAdapter(jobOfferList);
    mRecyclerView.setAdapter(adapter);
}
```

This solution queries the database in the background and asynchronously displays the result, but it is still far from perfect. We will iterate through the cursor to create a list of objects, and after this, we will send the list to the adapter, which is iterating over the list again to create the elements. What if we had an adapter that could build the list directly from the cursor? The solution to our problem exists, and it's called CursorAdapter. However, before moving to this, we need to implement the third method, which is still pending.

The third method, onLoaderReset, is called when the data is not valid. This could happen, for instance, if the source has changed. It removes the reference to the cursor, preventing memory leaks and is commonly used along with CursorAdapter. This one is the easiest of the three to implement. In our example, we can leave it empty; we won't have any memory leak because we will not use our cursor outside the method. If we were using CursorAdapter, there would be a reference to it outside our onLoadFinished method and we would need to set the adapter to null:

```
@Override
public void onLoaderReset(Loader<Cursor> loader) {
    //mAdapter.changeCursor(null);
}
```

RecyclerView and CursorAdapter

The CursorAdapter class creates an adapter based on a cursor and is intended to be used with ListsView. It extends from BaseAdapter.

The cursor passed to the adapter must have a column named _id. To do this, we don't need to change our database; we can simply rename the field from rowid to _id in the CursorLoader creation.

This is an example of a basic CursorAdapter:

```
SimpleCursorAdapter mAdapter =
new SimpleCursorAdapter(
   this,                // Current context
   R.layout.list_item,  // Layout for a single row
   null,                // No Cursor yet
   mFromColumns,        // Cursor columns to use
   mToFields,           // Layout fields to use
   0                    // No flags
);
```

Once it is created, we can pass it the new cursor in onLoadFinished:

```
mAdapter.changeCursor(cursor);
```

This solution is perfect if you are working with ListView; unfortunately, RecyclerView works with RecyclerView.Adapter and is not compatible with BaseAdapter. Therefore, the CursorLoader class can't be used with RecyclerViews.

At this point, we have two alternatives: one is to find an open source solution, such as CursorRecyclerAdapter (https://gist.github.com/quanturium/46541c81 aae2a916e31d#file-cursorrecycleradapter-java) and include this class in our app.

The second option is to create our own. To do this, we will create a JobOfferCursorAdapter class which extends from RecyclerView. Adapter<JobOffersAdapter.MyViewHolder>. This class, as with JobOfferAdapter, will have the onCreateView and onBindView methods. They are implemented in the same way, with the exception that the job offers are in a cursor and not in a list. To get JobOffer from a cursor row, we will create an extra method called getItem(int position). Apart from this, we need the getCount method, which will return the cursor size, and a changeCursor method, which will allow us to change the cursor in the adapter. Take a look at the following code:

```
public class JobOfferCursorAdapter extends RecyclerView.
Adapter<JobOfferCursorsAdapter.MyViewHolder>{
```

```
Cursor mDataCursor;

@Override
public int getItemCount() {
  return (mDataCursor == null) ? 0 : mDataCursor.getCount();
}


public void changeCursor(Cursor newCursor) {
  //If the cursors are the same do nothing
  if (mDataCursor == newCursor){
    return;
  }

  //Swap the cursors
  Cursor previous = mDataCursor;
  mDataCursor = newCursor;

  //Notify the Adapter to update the new data
  if (mDataCursor != null){
    this.notifyDataSetChanged();
  }

  //Close previous cursor
  if (previous != null) {
    previous.close();
  }
}


private JobOffer getItem(int position) {
  //To be implemented
  return null;
}


@Override
public JobOfferCursorAdapter.MyViewHolder
onCreateViewHolder(ViewGroup parent, int viewType) {
  //To be implemented
  return null;
}
```

```
@Override
public void onBindViewHolder(MyViewHolder holder, int position) {
  //To be implemented
}

private class MyViewHolder..


}
```

The getItem method needs to get JobOffer from a row in the cursor. To do this, we first need to move the cursor to this position with the moveToPosition(int position) method, and after this, we can extract the values for this row:

```
private Object getItem(int position) {
  mDataCursor.moveToPosition(position);
  return JobOffer.createJobOfferfromCursor(mDataCursor);
}
```

With this method ready, we can implement the rest of the functionality on the adapter based on the previous JobOffersAdapter:

```
@Override
public MyViewHolder onCreateViewHolder(ViewGroup parent, int viewType)
{
  View v = LayoutInflater.from(parent.getContext()).inflate(R.layout.
row_job_offer, parent, false);
  return new MyViewHolder(v);
}

@Override
public void onBindViewHolder(JobOfferCursorAdapter.MyViewHolder
holder, int position) {
  JobOffer jobOffer =  getItem(position);
  holder.textViewName.setText(jobOffer.getTitle());
  holder.textViewDescription.setText(jobOffer.getDescription());
}


public class MyViewHolder extends RecyclerView.ViewHolder implements
View.OnClickListener{

  public TextView textViewName;
  public TextView textViewDescription;
```

```
   public  MyViewHolder(View v){
      super(v);
      textViewName = (TextView)v.findViewById(R.id.rowJobOfferTitle);
      textViewDescription = (TextView)v.findViewById(R.
id.rowJobOfferDesc);
      v.setOnClickListener(this);
   }


   @Override
   public void onClick(View view) {
      Intent intent = new Intent(view.getContext(), OfferDetailActivity.
class);
      JobOffer selectedJobOffer = getItem(getAdapterPosition());
      intent.putExtra("job_title", selectedJobOffer.getTitle());
      intent.putExtra("job_description",selectedJobOffer.
getDescription());
      intent.putExtra("job_image",selectedJobOffer.getImageLink());
      view.getContext().startActivity(intent);
   }
}
```

With our own `CursorAdapter` adapted to `RecyclerView` completed, we are ready
to create the cursor and set the appropriate cursor when our loader manager has
finished. In `OncreateView`, we will retrieve new data from the server and upload the
view with the current data at the same time:

```
mAdapter = new JobOfferCursorAdapter();
mRecyclerView.setAdapter(mAdapter);

getLoaderManager().initLoader(MAA_LOADER, null, this);

retrieveJobOffers();

return view;
```

To display the data, we will change the cursor after the loader manager has finished:

```
@Override
public void onLoadFinished(Loader<Cursor> loader, Cursor cursor) {
  Log.d("ListFragment", "OnLoader Finished :" + cursor.getCount());
  mAdapter.changeCursor(cursor);
}

@Override
public void onLoaderReset(Loader<Cursor> loader) {
  mAdapter.changeCursor(null);
  Log.d("ListFragment", "OnLoader Reset :");
}
```

This works perfectly fine when there is previous data in the database. However, if we try to uninstall the app and run this the first time, we will see that the list is empty. Also, looking at the logs, we can see that we are storing the new job offers in the background correctly:

```
07-25 16:45:42.796  32059-32059/com.packtpub.masteringandroidapp D/
ListFragment: OnLoader Finished :0
07-25 16:45:43.507  32059-32059/com.packtpub.masteringandroidapp D/
ListFragment: Storing offers :7
```

What is happening here is that the changes in our database are not currently being detected, but this is very easy to fix when we use `CursorLoaders`. There is no need to manually register a content observer or restart the loader; we can set a listener in the cursor that `CursorLoader` uses and simply notify it when we make any change in the database. In our provider, we can set the notification URI to the cursor:

```
case JOIN_TABLE:
Cursor cursor =  mDB.query(DBOpenHelper.OFFER_JOIN_COMPANY, projection
,selection,selectionArgs,null,null,sortOrder);
cursor.setNotificationUri(getContext().getContentResolver(), uri);
return cursor;
```

Whenever the database changes, we can call:

```
Context.getContentResolver().notifyChange(Uri.parse(MAAProvider.JOIN_
TABLE_URI), null);
```

As a result, `CursorLoader` will automatically refresh the list. If we were doing the insert, update, or delete operations from the content provider, we could have had this line just before these operations to notify of any content change. In our example, we will simply add it manually after we have stored the new data in the database coming from Parse. You can use the following code for this:

```
public void done(List<JobOffer> jobOffersList, ParseException e) {
  Log.d("ListFragment","Storing offers :"+jobOffersList.size());
  MasteringAndroidDAO.getInstance().clearDB(getActivity());
  MasteringAndroidDAO.getInstance().storeOffers(getActivity(),
jobOffersList);
  getActivity().getContentResolver().notifyChange(Uri.parse
    (MAAProvider.JOIN_TABLE_URI), null);
}
```

We can now uninstall the App and install it again, and we will see that the list is empty for a few seconds while the offers are downloaded in the background. As soon as the download finishes, the cursor loader will refresh the list, and all the offers will appear. To put the icing on the cake, we will implement the *pull-to-refresh* feature.

Introducing pull to refresh with SwipeRefreshLayout

With this feature, the user can refresh the list at any time, by scrolling up when the list view is at the top. This is a popular feature seen in apps, such as Gmail and Facebook.

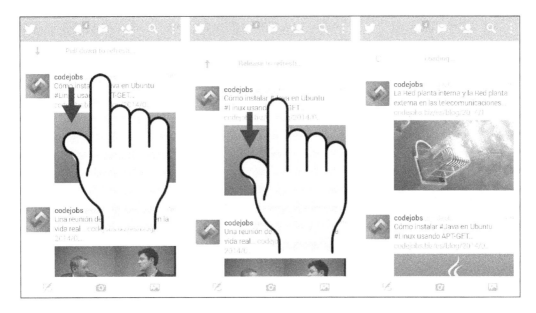

To achieve this functionality, Google released a component called `SwipeRefreshLayout`, which is included in the v4 support library. Prior to *revision 21* of this library, this was displayed as a horizontal line at the top of the screen that changed colors. Later, it was changed to a circle with a semicircle that rotates with the swipe movement.

To use this, we need to wrap our list with this element in the view:

```
<android.support.v4.widget.SwipeRefreshLayout xmlns:android="http://
schemas.android.com/apk/res/android" android:id="@+id/
swipeRefreshLayout" android:layout_width="match_parent"
android:layout_height="match_parent">

  <android.support.v7.widget.RecyclerView android:id="@+id/
my_recycler_view" android:scrollbars="vertical" android:layout_
width="match_parent" android:layout_height="match_parent" />
</android.support.v4.widget.SwipeRefreshLayout>
```

We can create a class variable called `mSwipeRefreshLayout` and set an `onRefresh` listener that will be called when the user wants to refresh:

```
mSwipeRefreshLayout = (SwipeRefreshLayout) view.findViewById(R.
id.swipeRefreshLayout);
mSwipeRefreshLayout.setOnRefreshListener(new SwipeRefreshLayout.
OnRefreshListener() {
  @Override
  public void onRefresh() {
    retrieveJobOffers();
  }
});
```

When the data is downloaded, we need to call `setRefresh` with the `false` value to stop the circle spinning forever:

```
@Override
public void done(List<JobOffer> jobOffersList, ParseException e) {
   Log.d("ListFragment","Storing offers :"+jobOffersList.size());
   MasteringAndroidDAO.getInstance().clearDB(getActivity());
   MasteringAndroidDAO.getInstance().storeOffers(getActivity(),
jobOffersList);
   getActivity().getContentResolver().notifyChange(Uri.
parse(MAAProvider.JOIN_TABLE_URI), null);
   mSwipeRefreshLayout.setRefreshing(false);
}
```

While refreshing, it should look similar to the following screenshot:

We can also change the colors of the arrow while rotating with the `SwipeRfreshLayout` and `setColorScheme()` methods. Just define three colors in the XML and set the three IDs of the different colors:

```
<resources>
  <color name="orange">#FF9900</color>
  <color name="green">#009900</color>
  <color name="blue">#000099</color>
</resources>

setColorSchemeResources(R.color.orange, R.color.green, R.color.blue);
```

We have achieved our goal. There is an easy way to test if the whole system works, from `SwipeToRefreshLayout` to the background Parse request, content provider, database, and cursor loader. We can open the app, and while we are on the list screen, we will go to Parse and create a new job offer, return to the app, and swipe to refresh. We should see the new job offer appearing after the refresh.

Summary

In this chapter, you learned how to create a database, use a database contract, and a database open helper. We saw the pattern of the DAO and made basic operations with it. Additionally, we replaced the DAO with a content provider, explaining how the URI matcher works and accessing it through a content resolver.

This allowed us to use `CursorLoader` with our own implementation of `CursorAdapter`, which is compatible with `RecyclerView`, to have a system where the UI is synchronized with the database. To finish the chapter, we saw how to use the popular feature, pull to refresh, to update the content on demand.

In the next chapter, we will take a look at how to add push notifications to our application as well as analytics services with an overview of the differences between the current analytics and push notification options available in the market.

9
Push Notifications and Analytics

We will start the chapter by talking about push notifications. You will learn how to implement custom solutions with notifications using Google Cloud Messaging, both on the server side and app side. Then, we will add notifications with Parse to our example. To finish with notifications, we will display our custom notifications using `NotificationCompat.`

In the second half of the chapter, we will talk about analytics. Having analytics to track what the user does in our app is essential to know how the user behaves, allowing us to identify patterns and improve the experience. We will implement one example with Parse and take an overview of the most popular solutions in the market.

- Push notifications
    - Sending and receiving with GCM
    - Notifications from Parse
    - NotificationCompat
- Analytics
    - Analytics with Parse
- Error report

Push notifications

Push notifications are important to engage users and provide real-time updates. They are useful to remind the user that there is an action pending. For instance, in the **Qkr!** app created by MasterCard, one can order food and drink in some restaurants, and if the user hasn't paid after a considerable period of time, they send a notification to remind the user that he/she needs to pay before leaving the restaurant.

They also work very well when we need to tell the user that we have new content or that other users have sent them a message. Any change that happens on the server side and requires informing the user is the perfect scenario to use notifications.

Notifications can also be sent locally from our own app; for example, we can schedule an alarm and show a notification. They don't necessarily have to be sent from a server.

They are shown at the top of the screen in the status bar, in a place called the notification area.

The minimum information required for a notification is an icon, a title, and detail text. With the arrival of material design, we can customize the notifications in different ways; for instance, we can add different actions to them:

If we scroll down from the top of the screen, we will show the notification drawer where we can see all the information displayed by the notifications:

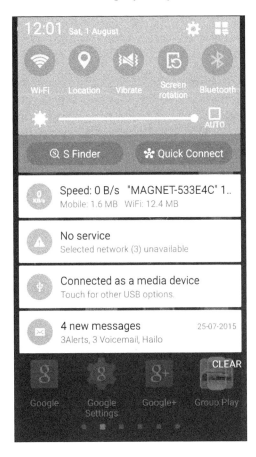

Notifications shouldn't be used as part of two-way channel communication. If our app needs constant communication with the server, as in the case of messaging apps, we should consider using sockets, XMPP, or any other messaging protocol. In theory, notifications are not reliable, and we can't control when exactly they will be received.

However, don't abuse notifications; they are a good reason for a user to uninstall your app. Try to keep them to a minimum and use them only when necessary.

You can assign a priority level to a notification, and Android Lollipop onward, you can filter the notifications you want to receive based on this priority level.

These are the key points and concepts you should have in mind while working with notifications. Before going into more theory, we will practice sending notifications to our app.

Sending and receiving notifications using GCM

There are different solutions on the market to send push notifications; one of these is Parse, which has a friendly control panel where anyone can easily send push notifications. We will use Parse as an example, but first, it's good to understand how this works internally and how we can build our own system to send notifications.

GCM (**Google Cloud Messaging**) uses push notifications, which we will send to our mobile. Google has servers called GCM connection servers that handle this process. If we want to send a push notification, we need to tell these servers first, and they will send it to our device later. We need to create a server or use a third-party server, which will communicate with the GCM servers over HTTP or XMPP as the communication can be done using both protocols.

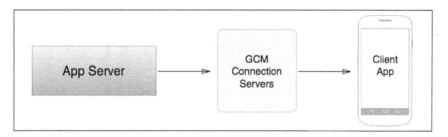

As we said earlier, we can't control exactly when a message is received because we have no control over the GCM server. It queues the message and dispatches it when the device is online.

To create our custom solution, the first thing we need to do is enable the messaging services on our app from the Google developers' website at `https://developers.google.com/mobile/add?platform=android`.

After you create the app, enable GCM messaging, and you will be provided with a Sender ID and a Server API Key. The sender ID was previously known as project number.

If we want to receive GCM messages, we need to register our client, which is our mobile app, with this project. To do this, our app will use the GCM API to register and obtain a token as confirmation. When this is done, the GCM servers will know that your device is ready to receive push notifications from this particular project/sender.

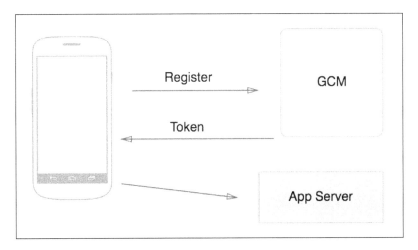

We need to add the play services to use this API:

```
compile "com.google.android.gms:play-services:7.5.+"
```

The registration is done through the **Instance ID** API, calling `instanceID.getToken` with the `SenderID` as a parameter:

```
InstanceID instanceID = InstanceID.getInstance(this);
String token = instanceID.getToken(getString(R.string.gcm_
defaultSenderId),
GoogleCloudMessaging.INSTANCE_ID_SCOPE, null);
```

We need to call this asynchronously and keep a Boolean variable in our app to remember whether we have been successfully registered. Our token can change with time, and we'll know when it happens with the `onRefreshToken()` callback. The token needs to be sent to our server:

```
@Override
public void onTokenRefresh() {
  //Get new token from Instance ID with the code above
  //Send new token to our Server
}
```

Once this is done, we need to create a `GCMListener` and add some permissions to the Android manifest:

```
<uses-permission android:name="android.permission.GET_ACCOUNTS" />
<uses-permission android:name="android.permission.WAKE_LOCK" />
<uses-permission android:name="com.google.android.c2dm.permission.
RECEIVE" />

<permission android:name="com.example.gcm.permission.C2D_MESSAGE"
  android:protectionLevel="signature" />
<uses-permission android:name="com.example.gcm.permission.C2D_MESSAGE"
/>

<application ...>
  <receiver
    android:name="com.google.android.gms.gcm.GcmReceiver"
    android:exported="true"
    android:permission="com.google.android.c2dm.permission.SEND" >
    <intent-filter>
      <action android:name="com.google.android.c2dm.intent.RECEIVE" />
      <category android:name="com.example.gcm" />
    </intent-filter>
  </receiver>
  <service
    android:name="com.example.MyGcmListenerService"
    android:exported="false" >
    <intent-filter>
      <action android:name="com.google.android.c2dm.intent.RECEIVE" />
    </intent-filter>
  </service>
  <service
    android:name="com.example.MyInstanceIDListenerService"
    android:exported="false">
    <intent-filter>
      <action android:name="com.google.android.gms.iid.InstanceID"/>
    </intent-filter>
  </service>
</application>

</manifest>
```

`GCMListener` will contain the `onMessageReceived` method, which will be called when we receive any message.

This is all we need from the client side; for the server side, we won't go into details in this book because it totally depends on the technology and the language chosen. There are different code snippets and scripts to send the notifications for Python, Grails, Java, and so on, which are easy to find on the Web.

We don't really need a server to send a notification because we can communicate directly with GCM. All we need to do is send a POST request to `https://gcm-http. googleapis.com/gcm/send`. This can easily be done using any online POST-sending service, such as `http://hurl.it` or Postman, a Google Chrome extension used to send network requests. This is how our request needs to look:

```
Content-Type:application/json
Authorization:key="SERVER_API_LEY"
{
  "to" : "RECEIVER_TOKEN"
  "data" : {
    "text":"Testing GCM"
  },
}
```

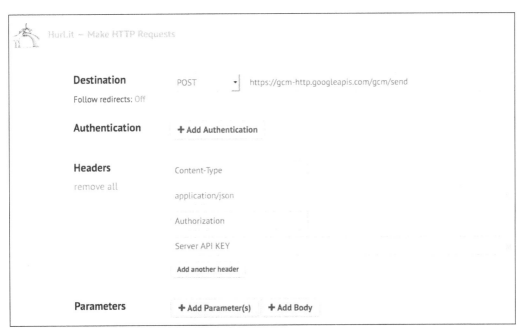

Continuing with `MasteringAndroidApp`, we will implement push notifications with Parse.

Push notifications with Parse

For our example, we will stick to Parse. The main reason is that we don't need to worry about the server side, and we don't have to create an app in the Google developer console with this solution. Another good reason is that it has a nice built-in control panel to send this notification, and we can target different users if we have been tracking users with different parameters in advance.

With Parse, we don't need to create a GCM listener. Instead, it uses a service that is already included in the Parse library, and we just need to register a subscriber for this service. All we need to do is add the permissions and receivers to our app, and we are ready to go:

```
<uses-permission android:name="android.permission.INTERNET" />
<uses-permission android:name="android.permission.ACCESS_NETWORK_
STATE" />
<uses-permission android:name="android.permission.WAKE_LOCK" />
<uses-permission android:name="android.permission.VIBRATE" />
<uses-permission android:name="android.permission.RECEIVE_BOOT_
COMPLETED" />
<uses-permission android:name="android.permission.GET_ACCOUNTS" />
<uses-permission android:name="com.google.android.c2dm.permission.
RECEIVE" />
<permission android:protectionLevel="signature"
android:name="com.packtub.masteringandroidapp.permission.C2D_MESSAGE"
/>
<uses-permission android:name="com.packtpub.masteringandroidapp.
permission.C2D_MESSAGE" />
```

Ensure that the last two permissions match your package name. The receivers need to go inside the `application` tag:

```xml
<service android:name="com.parse.PushService" />
<receiver android:name="com.parse.ParseBroadcastReceiver">
  <intent-filter>
    <action android:name="android.intent.action.BOOT_COMPLETED" />
    <action android:name="android.intent.action.USER_PRESENT" />
  </intent-filter>
</receiver>

<receiver android:name="com.parse.ParsePushBroadcastReceiver"
  android:exported="false">
  <intent-filter>
    <action android:name="com.parse.push.intent.RECEIVE" />
    <action android:name="com.parse.push.intent.DELETE" />
    <action android:name="com.parse.push.intent.OPEN" />
  </intent-filter>
</receiver>

<receiver android:name="com.parse.GcmBroadcastReceiver"
  android:permission="com.google.android.c2dm.permission.SEND">
  <intent-filter>
    <action android:name="com.google.android.c2dm.intent.RECEIVE" />
    <action android:name="com.google.android.c2dm.intent.REGISTRATION"
/>
    <category android:name="com.packtpub.masteringandroidapp" />
  </intent-filter>
</receiver>

</application>
```

To listen for notifications, we can register a subscriber in the `OnCreate` method of our `Application` class:

```java
ParsePush.subscribeInBackground("", new SaveCallback() {
  @Override
  public void done(com.parse.ParseException e) {
    if (e == null) {
      Log.d("com.parse.push", "successfully subscribed to the
broadcast channel.");
    } else {
      Log.e("com.parse.push", "failed to subscribe for push", e);
    }
  }
});
```

Now, it's ready. Simply go to the Parse web, select the **Push** tab, and click on **+ Send a push**. You can specify the audience, if you want to send it immediately or with a delay, and other parameters. It will keep a track of the push sent and indicate the people it was sent to.

If you see **1** in the **Pushes Sent** column and then take a look at the notification in your device, all is correct. The notification in your device should look as follows:

Using NotificationCompat

At the moment, we can see the default notification, which is created by the Parse receiver. However, we can set our own receiver and create nicer notifications with `NotificationCompat`. This component was introduced in the support v4 library, displaying notifications with the latest features in Android L and M as well as in previous versions until API 4.

In a few words, what we need to do is create a notification with the help of `NotificationCompat.Builder` and pass this notification to the system with `NotificationManager.notify()`:

```
public class MyNotificationReceiver  extends BroadcastReceiver {

   @Override
   public void onReceive(Context context, Intent intent) {
      Notification notification = new NotificationCompat.
Builder(context)
        .setContentTitle("Title")
        .setContentText("Text")
        .setSmallIcon(R.drawable.ic_launcher)
        .build();
```

```
    NotificationManagerCompat.from(context).notify(1231,notification);
  }

}
```

This will show our notification. The title, text, and icon are mandatory; if we don't add these three properties, the notification won't be shown. To start using our custom receiver, we need to specify in the manifest the register that we want to use, instead of the Parse push receiver:

```
receiver android:name="com.packtpub.masteringandroidapp.
MyNotificationReceiver" android:exported="false">
  <intent-filter>
    <action android:name="com.parse.push.intent.RECEIVE" />
    <action android:name="com.parse.push.intent.DELETE" />
    <action android:name="com.parse.push.intent.OPEN" />
  </intent-filter>
</receiver>
```

We discussed how to show custom notifications with `NotificationCompat`. Notifications have their own design guidelines, and they are an important part of material design. It is recommended to have a look at these guidelines and keep them in mind while using this component in your app.

 You can find the guidelines at `http://developer.android.com/design/patterns/notifications.html`.

The importance of analytics

It's very important to know what the user does with your app. Analytics help us understand which screens are most visited, which products the users buy in our app, and why certain users drop out during the registration process along with obtaining information pertaining to gender, location, age, and so on.

We can even track crashes that users have in our app along with information about the device model, android version, crash logs, and so on.

This data helps us improve user experience, for instance, if we see that the user is not behaving with the app as we anticipated. It helps define our product; if we have different features in our app, we can determine which is the most used. It helps us know the audience, which can be beneficial for marketing purposes. With crash reports, it's easier to keep the app free of bugs and crashes.

We will use Parse as an example to start tracking some events.

Analytics with Parse

Without adding any extra code and only with the `Parse.init()` method that we are already calling, we have some statistics in the Parse console under the **Analytics** tab.

In the **Audience** section, we can see the active installations and the active users displayed daily, weekly, and monthly. This is useful to understand how many users we have and how many of them are active. If we want to know how many uninstalled the app, we can look at the **Retention** section.

We will track some events and crashes to display information in these two sections, but first, we will take a look at **Explorer**. If you click on the **Explorer** button on the left, you should see the following option:

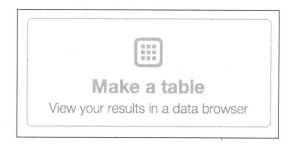

This will show a table where we can see different options to filter the data from our app. As soon as we start tracking events and actions, there will be more columns here, and we will be able to create complex queries.

By default, if we click on run query, we will see the following image of a table:

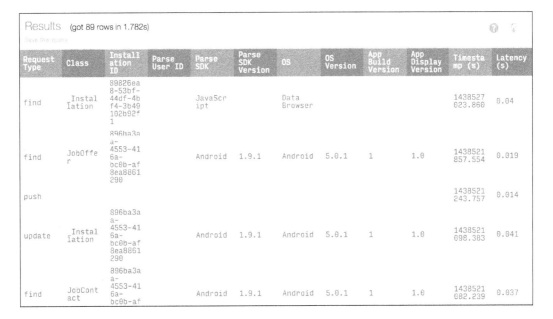

It shows all the information available under the default columns; no extra columns are needed for now. We can see all the different request types along with the OS, OS version, and version of our app.

We can work with the filter to produce different outputs. Some interesting outputs could be, for instance, sorting and grouping by app version so as to have an idea of how many people are using each version.

If we were using the same Parse database for different platforms, such as Android and iOS, we could filter by platform.

Here's an example of filtering by OS version, where we can see all the Android versions that our users are currently using:

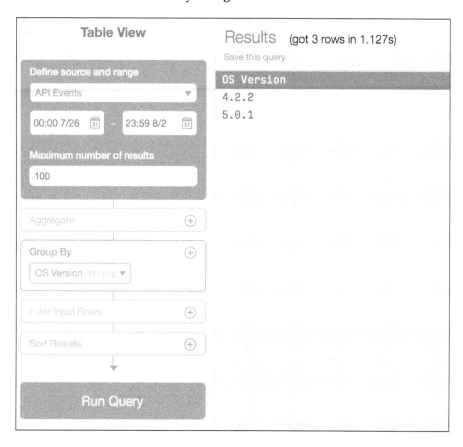

To gather more data about when and how often the app is opened, we can add the following line in the `oncreate` method of our splash screen or first activity.

```
ParseAnalytics.trackAppOpenedInBackground(getIntent());
```

This is an example of an event that we can track, but when we generally speak about event tracking, we refer to custom events. For example, if we want to track which job offer is the most visited, we will track an event in `JobOfferDetailActivity` with the title of the article visited. We can also track this event in the `onlick` listener when a row is clicked on to open the offer. There is no fixed rule for this; the implementations may vary. However, we need to know that the objective is to track the event when the offer is seen.

The code to choose the option where we track the event in the `OnCreate` method of `OfferDetailActivity` will look similar to the following code:

```
public class OfferDetailActivity extends AppCompatActivity {

    @Override
    protected void onCreate(Bundle savedInstanceState) {
        super.onCreate(savedInstanceState);
        setContentView(R.layout.activity_offer_detail);

        String job_title = getIntent().getStringExtra("job_title");

        Map<String, String> eventParams = new HashMap<>();
        eventParams.put("job_title", job_title);
        ParseAnalytics.trackEventInBackground("job_visited", eventParams);
```

The `trackEventInBackground` method launches a background thread to create the network upload request for us. The parameters are sent as a `Map` string with a maximum of eight.

If we visit different offers at different times and go to the analytics explorer section, we can easily create a query to see the number of times that each job offer was opened.

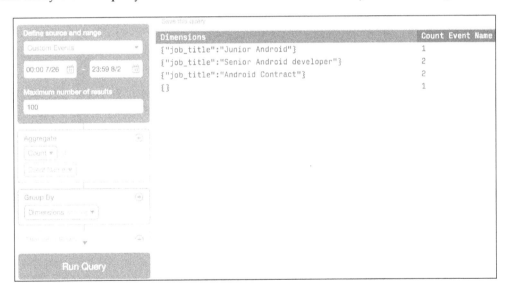

By grouping the data by dimension, which comprises the different parameters that we send with the event tracking, and using an aggregate of a count, we can get a count of every job offer visited.

Next, we will take a look at how to take advantage of this event tracking to use Parse as an error report tool.

The error report

Reporting crashes when our app is distributed is essential to maintain an app free of bugs and crashes. There are hundreds of Android devices on the market and different situations in which even the best QA person or tester would slip-up while releasing the app, and we end up with an app that crashes.

We need to assume that our app is going to crash. We must code as best as we can, but if a crash happens, we need to have the tools in place to report and fix it.

Parse allows us to track errors using the following code:

```
Map<String, String> dimensions = new HashMap<String, String>();
dimensions.put('code', Integer.toString(error.getCode()));
ParseAnalytics.trackEvent('error', dimensions);
```

However, this solution will only allow us to track errors in a controlled piece of code. For instance, let's say that we have a network request and it returns an error. This scenario can be handled easily; we just track the event with the error response from the server.

There is a problem when we have `NullPointerException` in our app, which is when we have a crash because something unexpected happened that we can't detect in the code. For instance, if the link of the image of a job is null and I try to read the link without checking whether the attribute is null or not, I will get `NullPointerException`, and the app will crash.

How can we track this if we do not control the part of the code where it happens? Fortunately, we have tools on the market that do this for us. HockeyApp is a tool that helps distribute beta versions and collect live crash reports. This is a tool that shows the error reports of our apps in a web panel. It's really easy to integrate; all we need is to add the following to the library:

```
compile 'net.hockeyapp.android:HockeySDK:3.5.0-b.4'
```

Then, we need to call the following method to report errors:

```
CrashManager.register(this, APP_ID);
```

The `APP_ID` would be found when you upload the APK to hockey or when you create a new app manually on the hockey website.

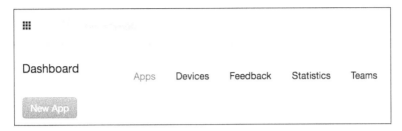

Once we know `App_ID` and register for crashes, if we have a crash, we will see a list with the number of occurrences, as in the following screenshot:

We'll finish with analytics by saying that Parse is just one of the alternatives; it's very common to use Google analytics as well, which is included in the Google Play service library. Google analytics allow us to create more complex reports, for instance funnel tracking to see how many users we drop during a long registration process, and we can see the data in different charts and histograms.

If you belong to a large organization, take a look at Adobe Omniture. It's an enterprise tool that helps you track different events as variables and then creates formulas to display these variables. It also allows you to combine your mobile analytics with data from other departments such as sales, marketing, and customer service. From my personal experience, the companies that I have seen using Omniture have a person working full time on the analytics study. In this case, all the developer needs to know is how to implement the SDK and track events; it's not a developer's task to create complex reports.

Summary

In this chapter, you learned how to add notifications to our app. We implemented push notifications with Parse and discussed how to create our custom notifications service using Google Cloud Messaging, with all the code needed on the client side and tools to test the server side. In the second half of the chapter, we introduced analytics, explaining why they are important, and tracked events with Parse. An important aspect in the analytics world is the error report. We tracked the errors in our apps using Parse and HockeyApp as well. To finish, we took an overview of other analytics solutions, such as Google Analytics and Adobe Omniture.

In the next chapter, we will work with location services and learn how to add `MapView` to our example, displaying a Google map with location markers.

10
Location Services

In this chapter, we will learn how to add a map view to our application using Google's Map Fragment. We will add markers onto the map, which will be used to point out locations of interest.

In order to do this, we will also discuss how to create a project in Google Developer Console and set up our application to use the Google Play Services SDK, which is required in order to use Google services in any Android application.

Every job offer has a location field in Parse; based on this, we will display markers on the map.

- Configuring the project
  - Getting the Google Maps API key
  - Configuring `AndroidManifest.xml`

- Adding the map
  - Creating the fragment for ViewPager
  - Implementing Map Fragment

- Adding a marker
  - Retrieving data from Parse
  - Displaying a marker for each location

- Adding a title

Configuring the project

In order for us to use the Google Play Service APIs, we need to set up our project with the Google Play Services SDK. If you have not already installed this, go to Android SDK Manager and get the Google Play Service SDK.

Now that our app uses Google Play services, to test the app, you must ensure that you run the app on either of the following:

1. An Android device with Android 2.3 or higher that has Google Play Store (Recommended).

2. An emulator that has Google Play Services set up. If you use Genymotion, **Google Play services** will not be installed by default:

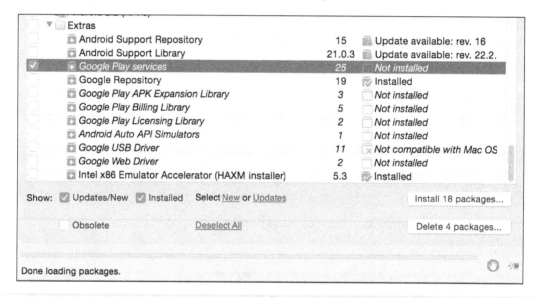

We need to make Google Play services APIs available to our app.

Open the app's `build.gradle` file and add the `play-services` library under dependencies. The line to add the `build.gradle` file should be similar to this:

```
compile 'com.google.android.gms:play-services:7.8.0'
```

Ensure that you change this to the latest version of `play-services` and update it when a new version is released.

Save the file and click on **Sync Project with Gradle Files**.

Getting the API key

For us to use the Google Maps API, we need to register our project with Google Developer Console and receive an API key, which we will then add to our app.

Firstly, we will need to get the SHA-1 fingerprint of our unique application. We can receive this from either the **debug certificate** or the **release certificate**.

- The **debug certificate** is created automatically when a debug build is done. This certificate must only be used for apps that are currently being tested. Do not publish an application using the debug certificate.

- The **release certificate** is made when a release build is done. The certificate can also be created using the **keytool** program. This certificate must be used when the app is ready to be released to Play Store.

Displaying the debug certificate fingerprint

- Find your debug keystore file with the name `debug.keystore`. This file is usually in the same directory as the Android Virtual Device files:

    ○ **OS X and Linux**: `~/.android/`

    ○ **Windows Vista and Windows 7**: `C:\Users\your_user_name\.android\`

- To show the SHA-1 fingerprint, open a terminal or command prompt window and enter the following:

    ○ **OS X and Linux**: We use the `keytool -list -v -keystore ~/.android/debug.keystore -alias androiddebugkey -storepass android -keypass android` command.

    ○ **Windows Vista and Windows 7**: We use the `keytool -list -v -keystore "%USERPROFILE%\.android\debug.keystore" -alias androiddebugkey -storepass android -keypass android` command.

After you enter the command, and press the *Enter* key, you will see an output similar to this:

```
Alias name: androiddebugkey
Creation date: Dec 16, 2014
Entry type: PrivateKeyEntry
Certificate chain length: 1
Certificate[1]:
```

```
Owner: CN=Android Debug, O=Android, C=US
Issuer: CN=Android Debug, O=Android, C=US
Serial number: 32f30c87
Valid from: Tue Dec 16 11:35:40 CAT 2014 until: Thu Dec 08 11:35:40
CAT 2044
Certificate fingerprints:
        MD5:   7E:06:3D:45:D7:1D:48:FE:96:88:18:20:0F:09:B8:2A
        SHA1: BD:24:B2:7C:DA:67:E5:80:78:1D:75:8C:C6:66:B3:D0:63:3E:
EE:84
        SHA256: E4:8C:BD:4A:24:CD:55:5C:0E:7A:1E:B7:FC:A3:9E:60:28:FB
:F7:20:C6:C0:E9:1A:C8:13:29:A6:F2:10:42:DB
        Signature algorithm name: SHA256withRSA
        Version: 3
```

Creating a Google Developer Console project

Go to `https://console.developers.google.com/project` and create an account if you haven't already done so. First, create a new project with your desired name. Once the project has been created, perform the following steps:

1. In the left sidebar, click on **APIs & auth** and then select the **APIs** option:

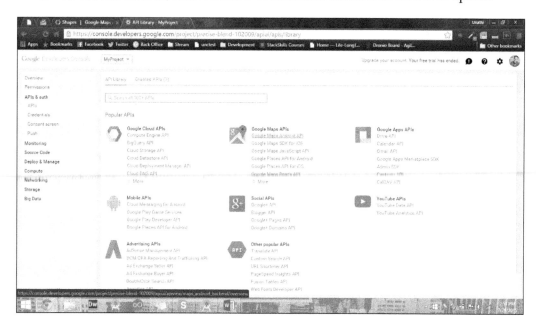

2. Select the **Google Maps Android API** and enable it.

3. Open **Credentials**, and click on **[Create new key]**.

4. Select **Android key** and enter your **SHA-1** fingerprint followed by your project's package name separated by a semicolon, as follows:

    ```
    BD:24:B2:7C:DA:67:E5:80:78:1D:75:8C:C6:66:B3:D0:63:3E:EE:84;com.
    packtpub.masteringandroidapp
    ```

5. Once you complete this, you will be able to view the credentials as in the following screenshot:

Configuring AndroidManifest.xml

Now that we have the API key for our Android application, we need to add it to our `AndroidManifest.xml` file.

Open your `AndroidManifest.xml` file and add the following code in the `<application>` element as a child:

```
<meta-data
    android:name="com.google.android.geo.API_KEY"
    android:value="API_KEY"/>
```

Replace `API_KEY` in the `value` attribute with the API key given on Google Developer Console.

We also need to add a few other settings to our `AndroidManifest`. Set the Google Play services version as follows:

```
<meta-data
    android:name="com.google.android.gms.version"
    android:value="@integer/google_play_services_version" />
```

Set required permissions as follows:

*   `INTERNET`: This permission is used to download map data from the Google Maps server.

*   `ACCESS_NETWORK_STATE`: This will allow the API to check the status of the connection to determine whether or not it will be able to download the data.

- `WRITE_EXTERNAL_STORAGE`: This will allow the API to cache the map data.
- `ACCESS_COARSE_LOCATION`: This lets the API retrieve the device's location using Wi-Fi or mobile data.
- `ACCESS_FINE_LOCATION`: This will give a more precise location than the `ACCESS_COARSE_LOCATION`, and it will also use GPS as well as Wi-Fi or mobile data. Take a look at the following code:

```
<uses-permission android:name="android.permission.INTERNET"/>
<uses-permission android:name="android.permission.ACCESS_NETWORK_
STATE"/>
<uses-permission android:name="android.permission.WRITE_EXTERNAL_
STORAGE"/>
<uses-permission android:name="android.permission.ACCESS_COARSE_
LOCATION"/>
<uses-permission android:name="android.permission.ACCESS_FINE_
LOCATION"/>
```

You also need to set up your OpenGL ES. The Maps API uses OpenGL ES to render the map, so it needs to be installed in order for the map to be displayed. To notify other services of the requirement and prevent devices that don't support OpenGL from showing your app on Google Play Store, add the following as a child of `<manifest>` in your `AndroidManifest.xml` file:

```
<uses-feature
  android:glEsVersion="0x00020000"
  android:required="true"/>
```

Your current `AndroidManifest.xml` file should be similar to the following code:

```
<?xml version="1.0" encoding="UTF-8"?>
<manifest xmlns:android="http://schemas.android.com/apk/res/android"
package="com.packtpub.masteringandroidapp">
    <uses-feature android:glEsVersion="0x00020000"
android:required="true" />
    <uses-permission android:name="android.permission.INTERNET" />
    <uses-permission android:name="android.permission.ACCESS_NETWORK_
STATE" />
    <uses-permission android:name="android.permission.WRITE_EXTERNAL_
STORAGE" />
    <uses-permission android:name="android.permission.ACCESS_COARSE_
LOCATION" />
    <uses-permission android:name="android.permission.ACCESS_FINE_
LOCATION" />
    <application android:name=".MAApplication"
android:allowBackup="true" android:icon="@drawable/ic_launcher"
android:label="@string/app_name" android:theme="@style/AppTheme">
```

```
    <activity android:name=".SplashActivity" android:label="@string/
app_name">
        <intent-filter>
            <action android:name="android.intent.action.MAIN" />
            <category android:name="android.intent.category.LAUNCHER" />
        </intent-filter>
    </activity>
    <activity android:name=".MainActivity" android:label="@string/
title_activity_main" />
    <activity android:name=".OfferDetailActivity" android:label="@
string/title_activity_offer_detail" />
    <provider android:name=".MAAProvider" android:authorities="com.
packtpub.masteringandroidapp.MAAProvider" />
    <meta-data android:name="com.google.android.geo.API_KEY"
android:value="AIzaSyC9o7cLdk_MIX_aQhaOLvoqYywK61bN0PQ" />
    <meta-data android:name="com.google.android.gms.version"
android:value="@integer/google_play_services_version" />
  </application>
</manifest>
```

Adding the map

Now that our application is configured for us to use map services, we can begin discussing how to add a visual map to our application. For the map, we will create another Fragment, which will be loaded on the second page of ViewPager.

There are two methods to display Google Map; either a MapFragment or a MapView object can represent it.

Adding the fragment

Create a new Java class within our fragments directory with the name MyMapFragment. The class should extend the Fragment type. Then, override the OnCreateView method and let it return the inflated view of fragment_my_map:

```
package com.packtpub.masteringandroidapp.fragments;

import …

/**
 * Created by Unathi on 7/29/2015.
 */
public class MyMapFragment extends Fragment {
```

```
    @Nullable
    @Override
    public View onCreateView(LayoutInflater inflater, ViewGroup
    container, Bundle savedInstanceState) {
        View view = inflater.inflate(R.layout.fragment_my_map, container,
    false);

        return view;
    }
}
```

Next, create the layout file for the fragment, and name it fragment_my_map. Set the root element of the layout to FrameLayout. We will temporarily add TextView to our layout just to verify that it works. The code for the fragment_my_map.xml file should be similar to this:

```
<?xml version="1.0" encoding="UTF-8"?>
<FrameLayout xmlns:android="http://schemas.android.com/apk/res/
android" android:layout_width="match_parent" android:layout_
height="match_parent">
    <TextView android:layout_width="wrap_content" android:layout_
height="wrap_content" android:text="This is a TextView"
android:layout_gravity="center" android:textSize="25dp" />
</FrameLayout>
```

The last step to add our fragment to the app will be editing the MyPagerAdapter. java file to display it as the second page. To do this, change the second case in the getItem method to return an instance of MyMapFragment as well as the page title in the second case of the getPageTitle method to return MAP:

```
@Override
public Fragment getItem(int i) {
    switch (i) {
        case 0 :
        return new ListFragment();
        case 1 :
        return new MyMapFragment();
        case 2 :
        return new SettingsFragment();
        default:
        return null;
    }
}
```

```
@Override
public CharSequence getPageTitle(int position) {
    switch (position) {
        case 0 :
        return "LIST";
        case 1 :
        return "MAP";
        case 2 :
        return "SETTINGS";
        default:
        return null;
    }
}
```

Now, when you run the app, the second page of the `ViewPager` should be replaced with our new fragment.

Implementing MapFragment

We will now use `MapFragment` to display a map on our app. We can do this by adding a `<fragment>` layout with `android:name` of `com.google.android.gms.maps.MapFragment`. Doing this will automatically add `MapFragment` to `activity`:

The following is the code for `fragment_my_map.xml`:

```xml
<?xml version="1.0" encoding="UTF-8"?>
<FrameLayout xmlns:android="http://schemas.android.com/apk/res/
android" android:layout_width="match_parent" android:layout_
height="match_parent">
  <fragment android:name="com.google.android.gms.maps.MapFragment"
android:id="@+id/map" android:layout_width="match_parent"
android:layout_height="match_parent" />
</FrameLayout>
```

Next, to be able to handle `MapFragment` that we added to our layout, we need to use `FragmentManager`, which we get from `getChildFragmentManager` to `findFragmentById`. This will be done in the `OnCreateView` method:

```java
FragmentManager fm = getChildFragmentManager();
mapFragment = (SupportMapFragment) fm.findFragmentById(R.id.map);
if (mapFragment == null) {
  mapFragment = SupportMapFragment.newInstance();
  fm.beginTransaction().add(R.id.map, mapFragment).commit();
}
```

We will allocate our fragment to `SupportMapFragment` instead of just `MapFragment` so that the application can support Android API levels lower than **12**. Use the following code:

The following is the code for `MyMapFragment.java`:

```java
public class MyMapFragment extends Fragment{

  private SupportMapFragment mapFragment;

  @Nullable
  @Override
  public View onCreateView(LayoutInflater inflater, ViewGroup
container, Bundle savedInstanceState) {
    View view = inflater.inflate(R.layout.fragment_my_map, container,
false);
```

```
    FragmentManager fm = getChildFragmentManager();
    mapFragment = (SupportMapFragment) fm.findFragmentById(R.id.map);
    if (mapFragment == null) {
      mapFragment = SupportMapFragment.newInstance();
      fm.beginTransaction().add(R.id.map, mapFragment).commit();
    }

    return view;
  }

}
```

Now, when we run the app, the map will be displayed on the screen.

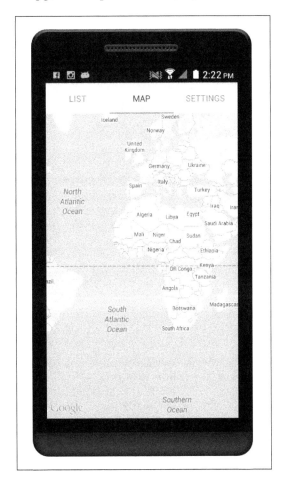

Adding a marker

The Google map is now visible, but it does not show any useful data for the user yet. To achieve this, we will add **map markers** to indicate points of interest for the user. These will be the locations of different job offers, which we will download from our Parse database.

We will also learn how to change the icon used to mark a point on the map to a custom image as well as have a title on the marker. This will make our app look more interesting and informative.

Retrieving data from Parse

Before we can display all our markers, we need to download all the necessary data from Parse.

In `MyMapFragment.java`, we will use `ParseQuery` to retrieve a list of the locations and use this to get the relevant information for each job offer before it is displayed. Perform the following steps:

- Create a private member variable named `googleMap` of the `GoogleMap` type and override the `onResume()` method.

- In `onResume()`, check whether or not `googleMap` is empty; if it is, this means that we have not yet added markers to the current instance of the map. If `googleMap` is empty, allocate the map from `MapFragment`, which we have already created. This is done using `getMap()`:

```
if (googleMap == null) {

  googleMap = MapFragment.getMap();

}
```

- Create a `ParseQuery`, which will retrieve all the data for the `JobOffer` table of our Parse database. Use the `findInBackground()` function with `FindCallback` so that we may begin processing the data only once it has all been downloaded. Use the following code:

```
ParseQuery<JobOffer> query = ParseQuery.getQuery("JobOffer");
query.findInBackground(new FindCallback<JobOffer>() {
  @Override
  public void done(List<JobOffer> list, ParseException e) {

  }
});
```

Displaying a marker for each location

Now, we will loop through the list of job offers received from Parse and use `addMarker()` to add a marker to `googleMap`. Perform the following steps:

1. When the `findInBackground` is done, create a `ParseGeoPoint` variable and a loop that will iterate each item on the list. We will use the `ParseGeoPoint` variable to store the coordinates from our Parse database:

   ```
   ParseGeoPoint geoPoint = new ParseGeoPoint();

   for(int i =0;i<list.size();i++){

   }
   ```

2. Within the loop, get the `GeoPoint` data from the list and save it to our `ParseGeoPoint` variable:

   ```
    geoPoint = list.get(i).getParseGeoPoint("coordinates");
   ```

3. Finally, add a marker to `googleMap` on each iteration with `addMarker()`:

   ```
   googleMap.addMarker(new MarkerOptions()
   .position(new LatLng(geoPoint.getLatitude(), geoPoint.
   getLongitude())));
   ```

Your `MyMapFragment.java` file should be similar to the following:

```java
public class MyMapFragment extends Fragment{

  private SupportMapFragment mapFragment;
  private GoogleMap googleMap;

  @Nullable
  @Override
  public View onCreateView(LayoutInflater inflater, ViewGroup
container, Bundle savedInstanceState) {
    View view = inflater.inflate(R.layout.fragment_my_map, container,
false);

    FragmentManager fm = getChildFragmentManager();
    mapFragment = (SupportMapFragment) fm.findFragmentById(R.id.map);
    if (mapFragment == null) {
      mapFragment = SupportMapFragment.newInstance();
      fm.beginTransaction().add(R.id.map, mapFragment).commit();
    }

    return view;
  }

  @Override
  public void onResume() {
```

```
      super.onResume();

  if (googleMap == null) {
    googleMap = mapFragment.getMap();

    ParseQuery<JobOffer> query = ParseQuery.getQuery("JobOffer");
    query.findInBackground(new FindCallback<JobOffer>() {
      @Override
      public void done(List<JobOffer> list, ParseException e) {

        ParseGeoPoint geoPoint;

        for(int i =0;i<list.size();i++){
          geoPoint = list.get(i).getParseGeoPoint("coordinates");

          googleMap.addMarker(new MarkerOptions()
          .position(new LatLng(geoPoint.getLatitude(), geoPoint.
getLongitude())));
        }

      }
    });

  }
 }
}
```

These markers should now be visible on the app:

Adding a title to a marker

What is useful about having a marker on the map isn't just showing a point, but also giving the user an easy and accessible way to get information about this location. We will do this by displaying a title on the marker when it is clicked on.

This can be achieved by simply adding `.title(string)` to our `addMarker()` method:

```
googleMap.addMarker(new MarkerOptions()
.position(new LatLng(geoPoint.getLatitude(), geoPoint.getLongitude()))
.title(list.get(i).getTitle()));
```

We now have a fully functioning display of a map that will show a title above the marker when a user clicks on it, as shown in the following image:

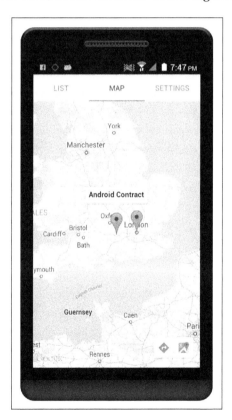

Summary

In this chapter, you learned how to add a map to our app. This required us to create a project on Google Developer Console and configure our app to access the API necessary. Once our app was completely configured, we moved on to adding the map to the view of our choice. We discussed handling a fragment within a fragment (MapFragment with our MyMapFragment). Although the single MapFragment could have been added individually by code, placing it within another fragment with a layout gives us the possibility of adding other UI widgets, such as FloatingActionButton, to the page if we need to. Finally, we made the map useful by displaying markers and information for locations, which we downloaded from Parse.

In the next chapter, you will learn how to debug and test our application.

11
Debugging and Testing on Android

In this chapter, you will learn how to debug in Android, an essential practice to save time in finding and fixing problems while developing our application.

We will learn how to create automated tests that can test the click of a button or the outcome of a single method. This is a set of tests that you can run in Android Studio to ensure that every time you develop a new feature, you don't break any of the existent ones.

You will also learn how to use **Robolectric** for unit tests and Espresso for integration tests.

At the end of the chapter, we will discuss how to test the UI with millions of random clicks using Monkey, how to record sequences of clicks through the app, and how to configure tests based on these recordings with MonkeyTalk.

- Logs and the debug mode
- Testing
  - ○ Unit tests with Robolectric
  - ○ Integration tests with Espresso
- UI Testing
  - ○ Random clicks with MonkeyRunner
  - ○ Recording clicks with MonkeyTalk
- Continuous Integration

Logs and the debug mode

We couldn't finish the book without mentioning logs and how to debug to solve problems while developing. Developing in Android can be more than just copying and pasting from Stack Overflow if you know how to solve your own problems.

The debug mode and logs are mechanisms used to help the developer identify where the problems are. With time, every developer improves and uses these techniques less frequently, but at the beginning, it's quite common to have an app full of logs. We don't want users to be able to see the log when the app is released, and we don't want to remove logs manually and then add them again when we release a new version. We will take a look at how to avoid this.

Working with logs

The log class is used to print out messages and errors, which we can read in real time using `LogCat`. This is an example of how to log a message:

```
Log.i("MyActivity", "Example of an info log");
```

The `Log` class has five methods, and they are used to have a different level of priority on the logs. This allows us to filter by priority in `LogCat`. There are situations when we display different logs, for instance, to see the number of job offers we download in every request. If we have a crash in our app, logs of the type error are our priority at this moment, and we want to hide other logs with less priority to find the error as soon as possible.

The five priorities are (from low to high) verbose, debug, information, warning, and error. (`Log.v` , `Log.d`, `Log.i`, `Log.w`, and `Log.e`)

We can filter by process with the bar at the top of the logging window. We can filter by priority and by keyword, and we can create custom filters by tag, process ID, and so on.

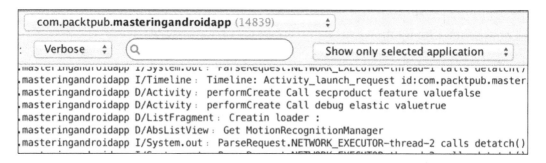

If the logs don't appear or they are old and not refreshing, try to open the dropdown to the right, select **No filters**, and then select **Show only selected application** again. This forces the console to refresh.

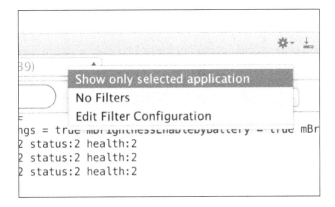

To finish with logs, we will create a wrapper and use a third-party library with the idea to be able to disable all the logs in the project by just changing the value of a Boolean. To do this, we simply create a class with the same methods of the Log class that depend on this Boolean value:

```
public class MyLogger {

    static final boolean LOG = false;

    public static void i(String tag, String string) {
        if (LOG) android.util.Log.i(tag, string);
    }

    public static void e(String tag, String string) {
        if (LOG) android.util.Log.e(tag, string);
    }
    ...
```

We need to use this wrapper every time we want to write a log — MyLogger.d() instead of Log.d(). This way, if we change the value of the Boolean LOG in the MyLogger class, it will stop all the logs in our project at the same time.

It is recommended to use the value from the BuildConfing.DEBUG variable:

```
    static final boolean LOG = BuildConfing.DEBUG;
```

This will be true if our app is in the debug mode, and it will be false when we release the app. So, we don't need to remember to turn the logs off in release mode, and there is no risk of a log appearing to the final user.

Using Timber, the log wrapper

Timber is a log wrapper created by Jake Wharton that takes the log to an advanced level, allowing us to have different log behaviors using the log tree concept. Take a look at the following code:

```
compile 'com.jakewharton.timber:timber:3.1.0'
```

One of the advantages of using timber is that we don't need to write a tag in our logs more than once in the same activity:

```
Timber.tag("LifeCycles");
Timber.d("Activity Created");
```

Our trees can have different behaviors; for instance, I might want to disable logs in the release mode, but I still want to handle errors; so, I will plant an error tree that will report the error to Parse:

```
if (BuildConfig.DEBUG) {
  Timber.plant(new Timber.DebugTree());
} else {
  Timber.plant(new CrashReportingTree());
}


/** A tree which logs important information for crash reporting. */
private static class CrashReportingTree extends Timber.Tree {
  @Override protected void log(int priority, String tag, String
message, Throwable t) {
    if (priority == Log.VERBOSE || priority == Log.DEBUG) {
      return;
    }
    //Track error to parse.com
  }
}
```

Debugging our app

Logs can be used to find problems while developing, but if we master the debug mode, we will find this practice much quicker.

While we are in the debug mode, we can set breakpoints in the code. With these breakpoints, we specify a line of code where we want the execution to stop to show us the values of the variables at that moment. To set a breakpoint, simply double-click on the left-hand side bar:

```
95
96                              @Override
97 ⚐        public void done(List<JobOffer> jobOffersList, ParseException e) {
98                  Log.d("ListFragment","Storing offers :"+jobOffersList.size());
99 ●              MasteringAndroidDAO.getInstance().clearDB(getActivity());
100             MasteringAndroidDAO.getInstance().storeOffers(getActivity(), jobO
101             getActivity().getContentResolver().notifyChange(Uri.parse(MAAProv
```

We set a debug point in the response of the method that gets the job offer. We can launch the debug mode from the top bar:

If we run the app in **Debug** mode, Android studio will pause the execution when it reaches this point:

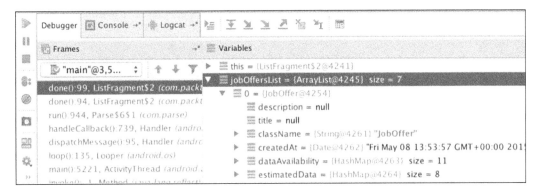

Android Studio will automatically prompt the **Debugger** window, where we will be able to see the variables at the point of execution. We can see in the preceding screenshot the job offer list and navigate to see what every offer has inside.

The important features here are the green **Play** button to the left, which continues the execution of our app until the next breakpoint, and the red square, which exits the debug mode and continues with the execution of the app.

We also have different controls available to move to the next line, into a method, or outside the method. For instance, consider that we have a breakpoint in the first line of the following command:

```
MasteringAndroidDAO.getInstance().clearDB(getActivity());
MasteringAndroidDAO.getInstance().storeOffers(getActivity(),
jobOffersList);
```

In this case, **Step Over**, which is the blue arrow pointing downward, will move our execution to the next line. If we click on **Step Into**, the blue arrow pointing to the bottom-right corner, we will get into the `getInstace()` method. With a combination of these controls, we can control the flow in realtime.

With the debug mode explained, we can now move on to automated tests.

Testing on Android

A new functionality is not complete without being tested first. We, as developers, have fallen many times into the trap of submitting code changes without writing a passing test first, only to find that the expected behavior was broken on future iterations.

We learned the hard way that writing tests boosts our productivity, increases code quality, and helps us release more often. For this reason, Android provided several tools to help us test our apps from the early stages.

In the following two sections, we will talk about my favorite setup, Robolectric for unit testing and Espresso for integration testing.

Unit tests with Robolectric

Until Robolectric, writing unit tests meant that we had to run them on a real device or an emulator. This process could take several minutes as Android build tools have to package the testing code, push it to the connected device, and then run it.

Robolectric alleviates this problem by enabling us to run our unit tests in the JVM of our workstation without the need for an Android device or emulator.

To include Robolectric using Gradle, we can add the following dependency to our `build.gradle` file:

```
testCompile "org.robolectric:robolectric:3.0"
```

We use `testCompile` to specify that we want this dependency to be included in our test project. For the test project, the default source directory is `src/test`.

Robolectric configuration

At the time of writing, Robolectric version 3.0 supports the following Android SDKs:

- Jelly Bean, SDK version 16
- Jelly Bean MR1, SDK version 17
- Jelly Bean MR2, SDK version 18
- KitKat, SDK version 19
- Lollipop, SDK version 21

By default, the tests will run against `targetSdkVersion` defined in the `AndroidManifest` file. If you want to run the tests against a different SDK version or if your current `targetSdkVersion` is not supported by Robolectric, you can override it manually using a properties file located at `src/test/resources/robolectric.properties` with the following content:

```
robolectric.properties
sdk=<SDK_VERSION>
```

Our first unit test

We'll begin by setting up a very simple and common scenario: a welcoming activity with a **Login** button that navigates the user to a login activity. The layout for the welcome activity is as follows:

```xml
<?xml version="1.0" encoding="UTF-8"?>
<LinearLayout xmlns:android="http://schemas.android.com/apk/res/
android" android:layout_width="match_parent" android:layout_
height="match_parent">
  <Button android:id="@+id/login" android:text="Login" android:layout_
width="wrap_content" android:layout_height="wrap_content" />
</LinearLayout>
```

On the `WelcomeActivity` class, we'll simply set the login button to start the login activity:

```java
public class WelcomeActivity extends Activity {

  @Override
  protected void onCreate(Bundle savedInstanceState) {
    super.onCreate(savedInstanceState);
    setContentView(R.layout.welcome_activity);

    View button = findViewById(R.id.login);
```

```
    button.setOnClickListener(new View.OnClickListener() {
      @Override
      public void onClick(View view) {
        startActivity(new Intent(WelcomeActivity.this, LoginActivity.
class));
      }
    });
  }
}
```

In order to test this, we can ensure that we start LoginActivity by sending the correct Intent. Because Robolectric is a unit-testing framework, LoginActivity will not actually be started, but we'll be able to check whether the framework captured the correct intent.

First, we will create the test file, WelcomeActivityTest.java, in the correct package within the src/test/java/ path. Robolectric depends on JUnit 4, so we will start by specifying Robolectric's Gradle test runner and some extra configuration that the framework will use to find the AndroidManifest resources and assets. Run the following command:

```
@RunWith(RobolectricGradleTestRunner.class)
@Config(constants = BuildConfig.class)
```

Now, we can write our first test. We'll begin by creating and bringing the welcome activity to the foreground:

```
WelcomeActivity activity = Robolectric.setupActivity(WelcomeActivity.
class);
```

Now that we have an instance of WelcomeActivity, it's easy to click on the login button:

```
activity.findViewById(R.id.login).performClick();
```

Finally, we have to verify that the framework captured the intent that would have started LoginActivity:

```
Intent expectedIntent = new Intent(activity, LoginActivity.class);
assertThat(shadowOf(activity).getNextStartedActivity(),
is(equalTo(expectedIntent)));
```

The `shadowOf` static method returns a `ShadowActivity` object that stores most of the interactions with the current activity under test. We need to use the `@Test` annotation, which tells JUnit that the method can be run as a test case. Putting everything together, we have the following test class (`WelcomeActivityTest.java`):

```
@RunWith(RobolectricGradleTestRunner.class)
@Config(constants = BuildConfig.class)
public class WelcomeActivityTest {

  @Test
  public void loginPress_startsLoginActivity() {
    WelcomeActivity activity = Robolectric.
setupActivity(WelcomeActivity.class);

    activity.findViewById(R.id.login).performClick();

    Intent expectedIntent = new Intent(activity, LoginActivity.class);
    assertThat(shadowOf(activity).getNextStartedActivity(),
is(equalTo(expectedIntent)));
  }
}
```

Running unit tests

Before being able to run the unit tests, we need to select the correct **Test Artifact** in Android Studio. To do so, we will open the **Build Variants** toolbar and select the **Unit Tests** artifact, as displayed in the following screenshot:

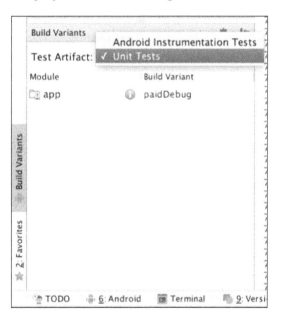

Now, from the **Project** window, we can run the tests by right-clicking on the test classes and selecting the **Run** option. Ensure that there are no spaces in the project path; otherwise, Robolectric will throw an exception prior to execution of the unit tests.

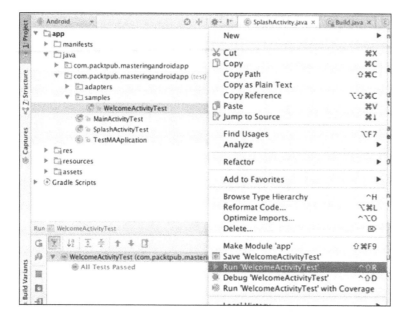

We can also run unit tests from the command line. To do so, call the `test` task command with the `--continue` option:

```
./gradlew test --continue
```

This option is ideal if we have a continuous integration system configured, such as Jenkins, Travis, or wercker.

This is the end of the Robolectric section. Next, we'll discuss integration testing with **Espresso**.

Integration tests with Espresso

Due to the very nature of Android and the vast amount of devices out there, we can never be certain of how the app might behave when we release it.

We naturally tend to manually test our app on as many different devices as possible, which is a tedious process that we have to repeat on every release that we do. In this section, we'll briefly discuss Espresso and how we can write tests that will run on a real device.

Espresso configuration

Before writing our first integration test, we need to install and configure our test environment. Perform the following steps:

1. From Android SDK Manager, we need to select and install **Android Support Repository** from the **Extras** folder, as shown in the following screenshot:

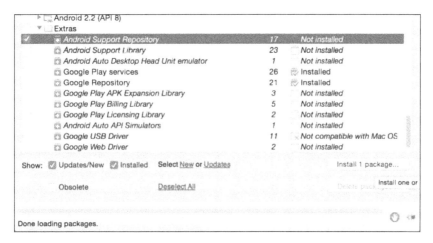

2. Create the folder for our integration tests code; this should be located at `app/src/androidTest`.

3. We'll also need to specify a few dependencies in the project's `build.gradle`. Use the following code:

```
dependencies {
   androidTestCompile 'com.android.support.test:runner:0.3'
   androidTestCompile 'com.android.support.test:rules:0.3'
   androidTestCompile 'com.android.support.test.espresso:espresso-core:2.2'
   androidTestCompile 'com.android.support.test.espresso:espresso-intents:2.2'
}
```

Recently, Android added support for JUnit 4 style test cases. To use this, we'll add `AndroidJUnitRunner` as the default test instrumentation runner in the `build.gradle` file:

```
android {
  defaultConfig {
    testInstrumentationRunner "android.support.test.runner.AndroidJUnitRunner"
  }
}
```

Writing an integration test

For this example, we'll continue from where we left off with Robolectric; we'll write a test for LoginActivity. For this activity, we'll set a simple layout with two EditTexts and a sign-in button. Run the following code (activity_login.xml):

```xml
<?xml version="1.0" encoding="utf-8"?>
<LinearLayout xmlns:android="http://schemas.android.com/apk/res/
android"
  android:orientation="vertical"
  android:layout_width="match_parent"
  android:layout_height="match_parent">

  <EditText
    android:id="@+id/input_username"
    android:layout_width="match_parent"
    android:layout_height="wrap_content"
    android:inputType="textEmailAddress" />

  <EditText
    android:id="@+id/input_password"
    android:layout_width="match_parent"
    android:layout_height="wrap_content"
    android:inputType="textPassword" />

  <Button
    android:id="@+id/button_signin"
    android:layout_width="wrap_content"
    android:layout_height="wrap_content"
    android:text="@string/signin"/>
</LinearLayout>
```

In LoginActivity, when the user clicks on the sign-in button, we'll send the credentials to the splash activity using the following code (LoginActivity.java):

```java
public class LoginActivity extends Activity {

  @Override
  protected void onCreate(Bundle savedInstanceState) {
    super.onCreate(savedInstanceState);

    setContentView(R.layout.activity_login);

    final EditText inputUsername = (EditText) findViewById(R.id.input_
username);
```

```
    final EditText inputPassword = (EditText) findViewById(R.id.input_
password);

    Button buttonLogin = (Button) findViewById(R.id.button_signin);

    buttonLogin.setOnClickListener(new View.OnClickListener() {
      @Override
      public void onClick(View v) {
        startActivity(new Intent(getApplicationContext(),
SplashActivity.class)
        .putExtra("username", inputUsername.getText().toString())
        .putExtra("password", inputPassword.getText().toString()));
        finish();
      }
    });
  }
}
```

For this test, we'll type the user credentials in the two input fields and verify that we bundle them correctly in the intent.

First, we will create the `LoginActivityTest.java` test file in the correct package within the `src/test/androidTest/` path. We'll use JUnit 4, so we will start by specifying the `AndroidJUnit4` test runner. Use the following command:

```
@RunWith(AndroidJUnit4.class)
```

Another distinction to Robolectric is that in Espresso, we need to specify a rule that will prepare the activity under test. For this, use the following command:

```
@Rule
public IntentsTestRule<LoginActivity> mActivityRule =
  new IntentsTestRule<>(LoginActivity.class);
```

Now, we can start writing the test. First, we'll need to type the login details in the two input fields:

```
String expectedUsername = "mastering@android.com";
String expectedPassword = "electric_sheep";

onView(withId(R.id.input_username)).perform(typeText(expectedUserna
me));
onView(withId(R.id.input_password)).perform(typeText(expectedPasswo
rd));
```

Then, we will send the intent by clicking on the sign-in button:

```
onView(withId(R.id.button_signin)).perform(click());
```

Finally, we have to verify that the captured intent contains the login credentials:

```
intended(hasExtras(allOf(
  hasEntry(equalTo("username"), equalTo(expectedUsername)),
  hasEntry(equalTo("password"), equalTo(expectedPassword)))));
```

Putting everything together, we will have the following test class (LoginActivityTest.java):

```
@RunWith(AndroidJUnit4.class)
public class LoginActivityTest {

  @Rule
  public IntentsTestRule<LoginActivity> mActivityRule =
  new IntentsTestRule<>(LoginActivity.class);

  @Test
  public void loginButtonPressed_sendsLoginCredentials() {
    String expectedUsername = "mastering@android.com";
    String expectedPassword = "electric_sheep";

    onView(withId(R.id.input_username)).perform(typeText(expectedUser
name));
    onView(withId(R.id.input_password)).perform(typeText(expectedPass
word));

    onView(withId(R.id.button_signin)).perform(click());

    intended(hasExtras(allOf(
    hasEntry(equalTo("username"), equalTo(expectedUsername)),
    hasEntry(equalTo("password"), equalTo(expectedPassword)))));
  }
}
```

Running integration tests

Similar to what we did with Robolectric, to run integration tests, we need to switch to the correct **Test Artifact** in Android Studio. To do so, we will open the **Build Variants** toolbar and select the **Android Instrumentation Tests** artifact:

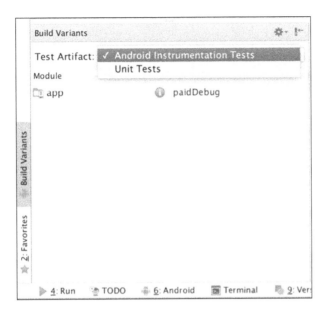

Now, from the **Project** window, we can run the tests by right-clicking on the test classes and selecting the **Run** option.

We can also run integration tests from the command line. To do so, we will call the connectedCheck (or cC) task:

```
./gradlew cC
```

Using a command line is the preferred way if we have a continuous integration system with a connected device or emulator. Once we write enough integration tests, we can easily deploy and run them on hundreds of real devices using services such as **Testdroid**.

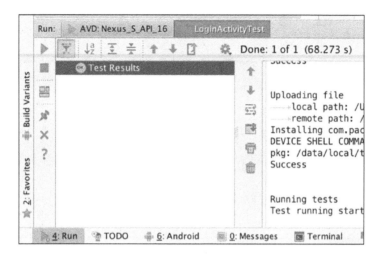

Testing from a UI perspective

The testing that we will do now is similar to the kind of tests that a person using the app could do. In fact, in companies that have **QA (Quality Assurance)**, people use these tools as a complement to manual testing.

UI tests can be automated as well, but they differ from unit and integration tests; these are actions performed on the screen, from clicking on a button to completing a registration process with recorded events.

We will start with stress testing using **The Monkey**.

Launching The Monkey

The Monkey is a program that can be launched from the command line with ADB. It generates random events in our device or emulator, and using a seed, we can reproduce the same random events. To clarify, let's consider an example with numbers. Imagine that I execute Monkey and it produces random numbers from 1 to 10; if I launched it again, I would get different numbers. When I execute The Monkey with a seed (this seed is a number), I get a set of different numbers from 1 to 10, and if I launch it again with the same seed, I will get the same numbers. This is useful because if we use a seed to generate random events and have a crash, we can fix this crash and run the same seed again to ensure that we fixed the problem.

These random events can vary from clicks and scroll gestures to system level events (such as volume up, volume down, screenshot, and so on) We can limit the number of the events and the type as well as the packages in which we run it.

The basic syntax in the terminal is the following command:

```
$ adb shell monkey [options] <event-count>
```

If you have never used ADB, you can find in it the `platform-tools` folder inside the Android SDK directory wherever it is installed in your system:

```
../sdk/platform tools/adb
```

When we open a terminal and navigate to this directory, we can write the following line of code:

```
adb shell monkey -p com.packtpub.masteringandroidapp -v 500
```

When you try to use `adb` and the output is `command not found`, you can restart `adb` with `adb kill-server`, `adb start-server`, and use `./adb` (*dot slash adb*) if you use Linux or Mac.

We can increase the number of events to `5000` or produce infinite events, but it is always recommended to set a limit of numbers; otherwise, you will have to restart the device to stop The Monkey. When you execute the command, you will be able to see the random events produced, and it will indicate the seed used in case you want to repeat the same chain of events:

```
:Sending Touch (ACTION_DOWN): 0:(959.0,1325.0)
:Sending Touch (ACTION_UP): 0:(962.4416,1320.4006)
    // Allowing start of Intent { cmp=com.packtpub.masteringandroidapp/.OfferDet
ailActivity } in package com.packtpub.masteringandroidapp
:Sending Touch (ACTION_DOWN): 0:(11.0,1461.0)
:Sending Touch (ACTION_UP): 0:(16.25062,1459.7925)
:Sending Touch (ACTION_DOWN): 0:(489.0,1583.0)
:Sending Touch (ACTION_UP): 0:(523.0899,1611.7065)
:Sending Touch (ACTION_DOWN): 0:(729.0,557.0)
:Sending Touch (ACTION_UP): 0:(730.1108,560.88055)
```

Depending on the app, we might need to adjust the time between events with the throttle milliseconds property in order to simulate a real user.

With the next testing tool, we will do a different kind of UI testing with the purpose of following a flow. An example of this would be if we have a registration process composed of three screens with different forms and want to record a test where a user fills up the form and continues through the three screens logically. In this case, The Monkey will not really help; with a very big number of events, it will eventually complete all the input fields with random characters and click on the buttons to move to the next screen, but this is not exactly what we want.

Recording UI tests with MonkeyTalk

The purpose of recording a sequence of tests such as the registration process is to have this test saved in order to be able to run it again when we make changes to our code. We might have to modify the network requests of the registration process without changing the UI, so these tests are perfect. We can just run them after finishing the modifications, and we don't have to manually complete the registration or fill the forms ourselves. We are not being lazy here; if we have hundreds of tests, this will be a lot of effort for one person. Also, with automated tests, we can ensure that the sequence of events is always the same.

MonkeyTalk is a free and open source tool, which comes in two versions; we'll be using the community version for our example.

 A list comparing the community and professional versions can be seen on their website at `https://www.cloudmonkeymobile.com/monkeytalk`.

MonkeyTalk can be used on real devices and emulators. It works by recording a list of events while we are in *Record mode*:

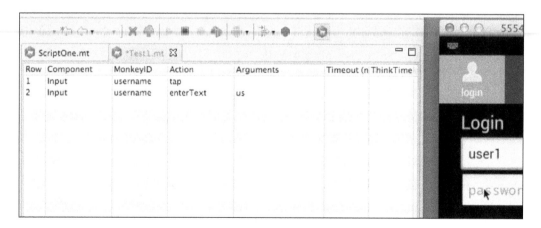

Once we enter this record mode by clicking on **Record** in the tool, every event will be recorded in an order, with the action performed and the argument used. In the preceding screenshot, we can see how tapping on `TextView` and writing some input on it are recoded as two events.

We could create this in a script file, and MonkeyTalk will reproduce it; so, we have the option to create our own sequence of events without recording. For the preceding events, we will write a script such as the following:

```
Input username tap
Input username enterText us
```

If we click on the **Play now** button, we will see all these steps executed on any device. We could record the scripts on an Android phone and play them on an iOS device.

Apart from recording and playing scripts, we can have verification commands. For instance, if we had a button that cleared all the input fields, we can add a verification command during the script using `currentValue`:

```
Input username tap
Input username enterText us
Input clearform click
Input currentvalue ""
```

This will report the result of the verification during execution, so we will be able to check whether all our verifications are passed correctly. For example, clicking on the button to clear the forms would need a click listener that clears every input text. If, for some reason, we make modifications and the IDs of the elements change, a MonkeyTalk test will report the problem with a command failed verification.

Wouldn't it be nice to have a tool that runs these UI tests for us, along with unit and integration tests, every time we make changes in our app? This solution exists, and it's called **Continuous Integration**.

Continuous integration

It is not our intention to explain how to build a continuous integration system because it's out of the scope of this book and it is not usually the job of an Android developer to set up the environment. However, you should be aware of what it is and how it works as it's directly related with Android.

A good suite of automated tests is always better combined with CI or a continuous integration solution. This solution will allow us to build and test our application every time there is a code change.

This is the way most companies with big projects work. If they have a team of developers, the code is usually shared in a repository, and they build a CI system connected to the repository. Every time a developer makes and commits a change to the repository, the collection of tests is executed, and if the result is successful, a new Android executable file (**APK**) is built.

This is done to minimize the risk of problems. In a big application, which takes years to be developed with different people working on it, it would be impossible for a new developer to start making changes without breaking or changing any of the existing features. This is because either not all the people in the project know what all the code is for, or the code is just so complex that modifying a component alters others.

 If you are interested in implementing this solution, we can point you to **Jenkins**, originally called Hudson at `https://wiki.jenkins-ci.org/display/JENKINS/Meet+Jenkins`.

Apart from testing and building our app, Jenkins will generate a test cover report, which will allow us to know the percentage of our code that is covered by unit and integration tests.

Summary

In this chapter, we started learning how to use logs in our app in an advanced way, and we took a quick overview of the debugging process. We explained what tests are and how to create unit and integration tests with Robolectric and Espresso, respectively.

We also created UI tests, starting with stress tests with the The Monkey, then generating random events, and later started testing with MonkeyTalk, recording event flows that can be played again verifying the output. To finish, we spoke about continuous integration to discover how companies put together the tests and the building system for an Android app.

In the next chapter, which is the last chapter of this book, we will take a look at how to monetize our app, how to build the app using different build flavors, and obfuscating the code, leaving it ready to be uploaded to App Store.

12

Monetization, the Build Process, and Release

This is the final chapter of the book; what we have left to do is monetize our app, generate different versions of it, and release and upload it to Play Store.

We will complete the build process by creating different build types and generating paid versions of the app without advertisements and a free version with advertisements. All of this will be in the same project but will be exported as two different apps.

Once the build process is finished, we will start implementing the advertisements and explain key points about advertisement monetization; this will make it possible to generate revenue using our application.

At the end, we will release the app and create an APK file of our APK signed with a release certificate, obfuscating the code so that it can be decompiled. We will upload it to Play Store and explain the key points to keep in mind during an app's publication.

- Build variants
- Monetization
    - Key points of advertisement monetization
    - Adding advertisements
- Releasing
    - Obfuscating and signing
    - Exporting with Gradle
- Uploading to Play Store

Using build variants

To explain how monetization with advertisements works on Android, we will add advertisements to our application, but before this, we will set up a build process that allows us to export two versions: the paid version and the free version. This strategy is commonly used in Play Store (having a free version with advertisements and a paid version without advertisements) so that all users can use the app for free, but the users that don't like advertisement and want to contribute with your app can always buy the paid version.

There is a second way of implementing this strategy, which is creating just one version and having the option of buying an add-on to remove the advertisements inside the app with In-App billing products. The downside of this way is that your app won't be listed in Play Store as a free app; it will be listed under "Offers in-App purchases", so there might be users who aren't comfortable with this or children that are not allowed by their parents to have paid apps or apps including payments. The second problem is that In-App billing is not easy to implement; the process is very complex with many steps involving setting up the service, creating the products in Play Store, consuming these products from the app, and setting up a test environment, where we can test the purchases without incurring charges. To show the build variants, we can navigate to **View** | **Tool Windows** | **Build Variants** or click on **Build Variants** in the left-hand side bar of Android Studio:

Build variants are a combination of build types and product flavors.

If we have the build types, A and B, and product flavors, 1 and 2, the outcome will be the following build variants:

```
A 1
A 2
B 1
B 2
```

To understand this better, we can see what build types and build flavors are and how to create them.

Creating build types

A build type allows us to configure the packaging of an app for debugging or release purposes.

Let's start by taking a look at our `build.gradle` file:

```
buildTypes {
  release {
    minifyEnabled false
    proguardFiles getDefaultProguardFile('proguard-android.txt'),
'proguard-rules.pro'
  }
}
```

In `build.gradle`, we can see that the build type release has two properties, which we will explain at the end of the chapter.

By default, we have two build types: **debug** and **release**. Even if we don't see the debug build type, all the variants will be generated in release and debug mode.

We can create more build types with different parameters; some of the parameters we can use are to:

- Sign the configuration
- Debug the signing flag
- Change the version name or package name suffix

This means that we can have different types signed with different certificates with the debug mode enabled or false and with a different package name.

The build type is not intended to create a different version of our app, such as demo or full, free or paid, and so on. For this, we have product flavors. Every build type is applied to every build flavor, creating a build variant as we saw before.

Product flavors

We will create two product flavors and declare them in `build.gradle` using the following code:

```
productFlavors {
  paid {
    applicationId "com.packtpub.masteringandroidapp"
  }
  free {
    applicationId "com.packtpub.masteringandroidapp.free"
  }
}
```

We have a paid flavor, which is the app without advertisements, and a flavor called *free*, which is the free version with advertisements. For each product flavor, we can create a folder at the `../src/` level of our project. We don't need a folder for our paid version as it will be main by default.

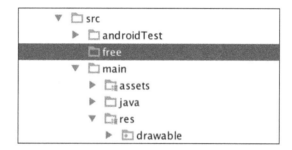

This way, we can have different classes and resources for each build, even a different `AndroidManifest.xml` file. Our app will share the common code between the paid and the free versions in the `main` folder, with a specific code for ads in the `free` folder.

To switch between the different versions, we can simply change the dropdown in the build variant window, as in the following screenshot:

Once a build variant is selected, we can either run the app or export it, and it will run or export the selected flavor accordingly. These can be configured to have a different package name and a different version name.

Now, we will take a look at how to add a specific code to the free version that won't be included in the main paid version.

Monetization in Android

We will describe the three common ways to earn money through an application.

Firstly, we can sell the application for a price in Play Store. There are some cases where charging for your app makes more sense than providing a free app with adverts or in-app products. If you create an app with big value for a small amount of users, you should definitely think about this option. For instance, if we were to release an app to professionally design houses for architects, we would know that our app will not be downloaded by millions of users; it's for a specific and targeted audience looking for quality software. We won't make enough profit with advertisements and our users will be keen to pay a good amount for software that makes their job easier. There is always a risk in asking for the money up front; even if the user has the option to obtain a refund for the app, he/she might not be attracted enough to try it. That is why we should consider the second model.

The second option is known as a **freemium** model. We release a free app but include in-app purchases in it. Applied to the same example of an app to design houses, we could offer three designs for free so that when the user is comfortable with our product, we can ask him/her to purchase a one-time license or a subscription to continue using the app. It's very common in games, where you can purchase items for your character. It is in games where we can see how this model can also be combined with the third model to get the maximum revenue possible.

The third model of monetization is the **advertisement model**; we place adverts in our apps, and when the user clicks on them, we get revenue. We can use different types of advertisements—from full screen advertisements to small banners at the bottom. We'll focus on this model. Implementing it is easier than you can imagine. But before implementing it, we need to explain what terms such as **CPC** (**Cost Per Click**), **CTR** (**Click Through Rate**), fill rate, and so on mean, which will help us choose a good advertisement platform and provider. This is also necessary to understand the metrics and be able to read the charts to know how the advertisements in your app are performing. Having advertisements in different places can change the revenue; however, we need to maximize the revenue without annoying the user. If we offer the user the option to remove advertisements for a small amount of money with an in-app product or with a paid version without advertisements, we can increase the number of advertisements. It's best for the user if they know that they have a choice. If they choose to live with the advertisements, it's their decision, and it won't annoy them as much as if we placed a lot of advertisements without the option to remove them.

Key points in advertisement monetization

We will explain the basics to understand how advertisement monetization works. There are a few concepts in the business with abbreviations that can be confusing at first.

Once we register with an advertisement platform, we will see a reports page with stats about our app. Here is an example of the dashboard from the advertisement network, `AdToApp`:

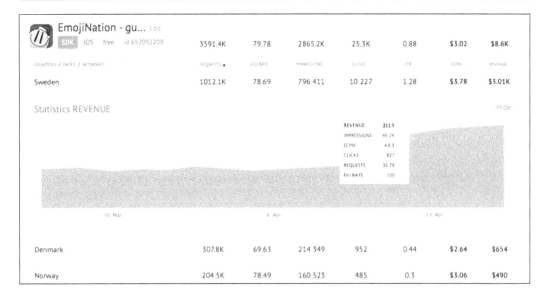

EmojiNation - gu... Edit							
50K iOS free id 652092209	3591.4K	79.78	2865.2K	25.3K	0.88	$3.02	$8.6K
COUNTRIES / DATES / NETWORKS	REQUESTS ▾	FILLRATE	IMPRESSIONS	CLICKS	CTR	ECPM	REVENUE
Sweden	1012.1K	78.69	796 411	10 227	1.28	$3.78	$3.01K

Statistics REVENUE   Hide

REVENUE:	211 $
IMPRESSIONS	46.2K
ECPM	4.8 $
CLICKS	827
REQUESTS	36.79
FILLRATE	100

10. Mar   6. Apr   13. Apr

| Denmark | 307.8K | 69.63 | 214 349 | 952 | 0.44 | $2.64 | $654 |
| Norway | 204.5K | 78.49 | 160 523 | 485 | 0.3 | $3.06 | $490 |

Here, we can see requests, fill rate, impressions, clicks, CTR, eCPM, and revenue. Let´s consider each of them.

Requests mean the number of times our app asked the advertisement network for an advert. For instance, if we decide to add a full screen advertisement at the start of our app, every time we start the app, there will be a request to the server to get back an advertisement.

We don't have the advertisement inside our app; what we have is a placeholder, a frame, and an `AdView`, which will be filled with content provided by the advertisement network. Sometimes, the advertising network doesn't have an ad for us at the moment of the request, which is why the next concept is important.

Fill rate is a percentage derived by the amount of delivered ads divided by the amount of requested ads. For instance, if we start our app ten times and only get back adverts five times, we will have a fill rate of 50 percent. What we want in a good ad network is a fill rate of 100 percent. We want to show as many ads as possible and with a good CPC.

CPC, or cost per click, is how much we earn each time a user clicks on an advertisement in our app; the higher it is, the most revenue we get. The advertiser determines the CPC for an advertisement. Some advertisers may be willing to pay more per click than others.

Many clicks with low CPC is not necessarily better than a few clicks with high CPC. That's why the quality of the advertisements that we have is important.

Impressions are how many times an advertisement is shown to the user. In the previous example, with ten advertisement requests and five failed, we would have five impressions. Impressions don't generate revenue if the user doesn't click on them.

Clicks are the number of times a user clicks on an advertisement. This is what generates the revenue based on the CPC. So, five clicks with a 0.5$ CPC will generate 5x0.5, which is 2.5$.

CTR, or click through rate, is the percentage given by the amount of clicks that your app receives divided by the amount of impressions. If we have 100 advertisements and one click, our CTR will be 1 percent. This amount is generally under 5 percent; users don't click on every advertisement they see, and you could have problems with an advertisement platform, such as **Admob**, cancelling your account and payments if they believe you are cheating by forcing the user to click on the advertisement. Let's say that we show a dialog at the start of our app and ask the user to click on an advertisement to continue using our app. This will basically give us 100 percent CTR; for every impression, there will be a click, and this is not allowed. We can't, under any circumstances, promote a click.

Advertisement providers want their advertisement to be seen by someone interested in it; they don't want to pay for the click of a person not interested in their advertisement, who will close it after a second. It could be that you have a high CTR because you have a good spot in your app and the advertisements are of interest to every user. If this happens, you will have to explain to your advertisement network, or some, such as **Admob**, will shut down your account. But we shouldn't be too unfair to them; they do this because they have found a lot of people trying to break the rules, and such a massive company can't focus on individuals, so they need to have objective filters.

Other advertisement network companies are more flexible with this; they usually assign an agent to you, who you can contact frequently on Skype or e-mail, and in case of any problem, they usually let you know.

eCPM stands for "effective cost per thousand impressions". It is calculated by dividing the total earnings by the total number of impressions in thousands. This is basically a quick way of knowing how good you are doing just by looking at a number — very useful to compare advertisement networks. It's a number usually between $0 and 3$.

We need to consider that this does not include the fill rate. It is the cost per thousand impressions and not per thousands requests. A three dollar eCPM with a 50 percent fill rate is the same as one and a half dollar eCPM with 100 percent fill rate.

What makes an advertisement network good is a high fill rate with a high eCPM. We need both to be high; adverts with expensive clicks and not enough fill rates won't produce any revenue because they simply won't be shown.

The guys from **AdToApp** created a good graphic explaining this:

This graphic represents what we have been talking about; a premium advertisement network with a very high eCPM and a low fill rate is represented as a tall but empty building with the lights off.

We are finished with the theory, and we can start integrating an advertisement solution; in this case, we will choose AdToApp.

Adding advertisements with AdToApp

There is no way to know which advertisement provider is better for you; the best you can do is to try different ones and have a look at the stats.

From experience, we like to use AddToApp because apart from the good delivery results, it's really easy to integrate, and it can be included in your app even if you have another network. Therefore, it's really easy to measure its performance.

It's ideal to use in this book with `MasteringAndroidApp` as it allows us to use different types of advertisements, full screen advertisements, banners, videos, and so on.

There are mediators for more than 20 different advertisement networks, so including their SDK, we will have access to plenty of advertisements with a high fill rate guaranteed. Regarding their eCPM, they analyze which network is giving better results for you; so, if they can deliver advertisements from multiple networks, they will deliver the ones with better results.

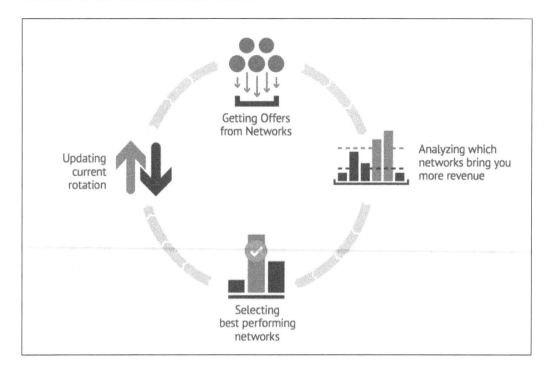

We can start creating an account at `https://adtoapp.com/?r=OZ-kU-W9Q2qeMmdJsaj3Ow`.

Once the account is created, we will create an app using the package name of our app.

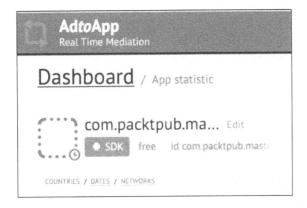

We will click on the SDK button to download their SDK and get configuration values for the integration.

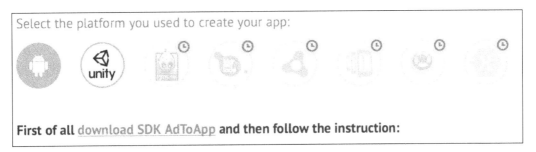

The integration is straightforward; the SDK will contain an `AdToAppSDK.jar` file, which we need to copy into `libs`. We need to add Google Play Services in `build.gradle` and the support library *v7*, but we already have this.

We need to add the basic permissions to the manifest, which we already have as well, using the following code:

```
<uses-permission android:name="android.permission.INTERNET" />
<uses-permission android:name="android.permission.ACCESS_NETWORK_
STATE" />
<uses-permission android:name="android.permission.WRITE_EXTERNAL_
STORAGE" />
<uses-permission android:name="android.permission.READ_PHONE_STATE" />
```

Then, we need to add extra mandatory assets in the manifest, which can be copied from the same website; it contains the keys of our account. You can find them under the first section, as shown in the following screenshot:

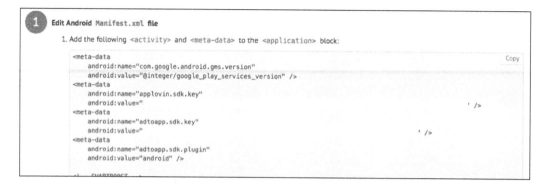

Lastly, we can take a look at how to implement **Interstitials & Banners** or rewarded ads. Rewarded advertisements are the type of advertisements that pop up in a game and say, *Watch this video and get (gold, gems, and so on)*. The viewing of these advertisements is totally up to the users if they want the reward:

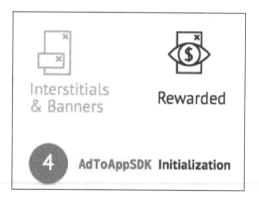

If we choose interstitials and banners, we need to initialize them depending on whether we want only video advertisements, only images (banners), or both images and videos in an interstitial.

In the website, depending on the type of advert you want, the necessary code will be shown.

The SDK is really flexible; we can go further and set callbacks to know when the banners were loaded and clicked on. This allows us to track the number of clicks in our advertisements and verify that they are the same as in the AdToApp console, making the process transparent.

If we need extra help, we can activate logs in the SDK, which will inform us in case of any problem.

Now, remember the good practices we mentioned at the start of the section about maximizing the number of advertisements without disturbing the user too much and implementing them in your app to start getting revenue!

Releasing our app to Play Store

Finally, our app is ready! This is the best moment while developing a new app; it is time to upload it to Play Store, get feedback from users, and hopefully get thousands of downloads.

We need to export the app to an APK file; in order to be uploaded to Play Store, it has to be signed with a release certificate. This point is very important; once an application is signed with a certificate, if we upload it to Play Store and want to upload a new version in the future, it has to be signed with the same certificate.

This certificate will be created by us during the release process. It needs an alias and a password, so ensure that you remember these details and save the certificate file in a safe place. Otherwise, say your app gets good ratings and a good number of downloads, and you want to update the version, but you don't have your certificate or have forgotten the password. In this case, you won't be able to update, you will have to upload a new app with a different package name, and it will start with zero downloads and zero ratings.

Code obfuscation

Another important thing to take into consideration while releasing the app is code obfuscation. If we export the app without obfuscating the code, anyone can download the APK and decompile it, allowing them to see your code, which can be a security problem if you have Parse IDs, server access details, a GCM project number, and so on in it.

We can obfuscate the code using **Proguard**. Proguard is a tool included in the Android build system. It obfuscates, shrinks, and optimizes the code, removing unused code and renaming classes, fields, and methods to prevent reverse engineering.

Beware of this renaming of classes and methods; it can affect your crash and error reports as the stack trace will be obfuscated. However, this is not a problem as we can retrace them with a mapping file that we will save while releasing the app, which will allow us to convert the crash and report to readable and not obfuscated code.

To activate Proguard, we need to set the `minifyEnabled` property to `true` in `buildTypes`. You can execute the following code for this:

```
buildTypes {
  release {
    minifyEnabled true
    proguardFiles getDefaultProguardFile('proguard-android.txt'),
'proguard-rules.pro'
  }
}
```

In our project, we have a `proguard-rules.pro` file, where we can add the rules to be considered while obfuscating. For instance, some third-party libraries cannot work properly if we obfuscate them, and there is no risk in leaving these libraries without obfuscation as they are not something that we created; we just added them to our project.

To prevent a third-party library from being obfuscated, we can add the rule `-keep` along with the rule and `-dontwarn` to ignore warnings. For instance, we added `calligraphy` to use custom fonts; this is how we can ignore it during the obfuscation:

```
# DONT OBFUSCATE EXTERNAL LIBRARIES

# CALLIGRAPHY
-dontwarn uk.co.chrisjenx.calligraphy.**
-keep class uk.co.chrisjenx.calligraphy.** {*;}
# TIMBER
-dontwarn timber.log.**
-keep class timber.log.** {*;}
```

Using `keep` and the name of the package, we will keep all the classes inside this package.

We will add Proguard in the debug mode to create a crash intentionally and see how the stack trace looks obfuscated:

```
Caused by: java.lang.NullPointerException: Attempt to invoke virtual
method 'void android.view.View.setVisibility(int)' on a null object
reference
          at com.packtpub.masteringandroidapp.SplashActivity.
onCreate(Unknown Source)
```

We can copy this `stracktrace` in a text file and go to `app/build/outputs/ mapping/product_flavor_name/ release_or_debug/mapping.txt` to get our `mapping.txt` file.

Consider that we execute the retrace command in `<sdk_root>/tools/proguard` with the following code:

```
retrace.sh [-verbose] mapping.txt [<stacktrace_file>]
```

In this case, we will have the crash in the correct line, as follows:

```
Caused by: java.lang.NullPointerException: Attempt to invoke virtual
method 'void android.view.View.setVisibility(int)' on a null object
reference
at com.packtpub.masteringandroidapp.SplashActivity.
onCreate(SplashActivity.java:21)
at android.app.Activity.performCreate(Activity.java:6289)
```

Remember to save a copy of `mapping.txt` with every release of your app; this file is overwritten every time we release it, so it's very important to save the file at the moment of every release. Alternatively, if you have a repository and you tag the commits for every release, you can go back and generate the same release again, which will have the same mapping file in theory.

Now that we have our app protected against reverse engineering, we can continue with the release process.

Exporting the app

When we export an application, what we do is create an APK file in the release mode and sign it with a certificate. This certificate is proof that an app in Play Store is ours, and with it, we can upload the same app as we explained before. We will export the app and create a certificate this time.

To export our application, we have two ways: one way is to use Gradle and the terminal inside Android Studio and the second way is to use the wizard in Android Studio. We will see both, but let's create the certificate using the second way first.

Navigate to **Build | Generate Signed Apk**; you will see a dialog similar to the following:

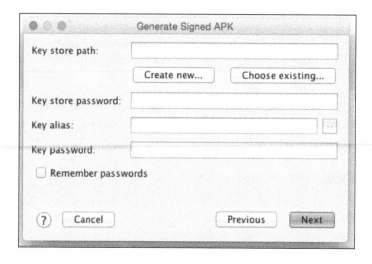

If we have exported this app before and created a certificate for it then, we just need to select a path and insert the alias and password, and this will export a new version of the app signed with the existing certificate.

For us, this is the first time that we are exporting MasteringAndroidApp, so we will click on **Create new....**. On the next screen, we need to select the path where will save the certificate, which is a .keystore file.

We also need a password for the keystore and a password for the alias inside the certificate. For a date with validity, 100 years will be okay; if your app lives more than you, it won't be your problem! Finally, some personal information in at least one field is required here:

Finally, it will ask us which flavor we want to export, and it will create the .apk, pointing to us the path of the file.

This way is straightforward, but there is an automated way to export the app using the command line and Gradle; it's very useful if we want to build the app with Jenkins, for instance.

To do this, we need to add a signing configuration in `build.gradle` so that when the app is generated automatically, it will know which `keystore` and which alias and passwords to use. The following code will help in doing this:

```
signingConfigs {
  release {
    storeFile file("certificate.keystore")
    storePassword "android"
    keyAlias "android"
    keyPassword "android"
  }
}
```

There is no need to say that this can lead to a security problem; the password is written in `build.gradle` and the certificate file is included in our project. If we do this, we need to keep the project safe. If this is a concern, you can read the password and the alias at runtime with the following code:

```
storePassword new String(System.console().readPassword("\n\$ Enter
keystore password: "))
keyAlias System.console().readLine("\n\$ Enter key alias: ")
keyPassword new String(System.console().readPassword("\n\$ Enter key
password: "))
```

When we run the command to generate the signed APK, it will ask us for the password alias and alias password. We can use the following line of code for this:

```
>./gradlew assembleRelease
```

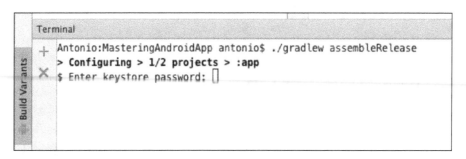

With our app exported, we can proceed to the last step: uploading to Play Store.

Uploading our app to Play Store

To publish an app, we need a Google developer account. If you don't have one, you can obtain one from `https://play.google.com/apps/publish/`.

Creating a publisher account

The first step to creating a publisher account is to enter the basic information and read and accept the developer distribution agreement. The second step is the payment of a development license fee of 25 dollars for the creation of the account. This is all we have to pay to publish an app, and it's paid just a single time—one single payment for a lifetime's license. We can't complain, considering in iOS, the fee is 99 dollars yearly.

The final and third step needs the developer's name, which will appear under the name of our application. Take a look at the following example in Google Inc:

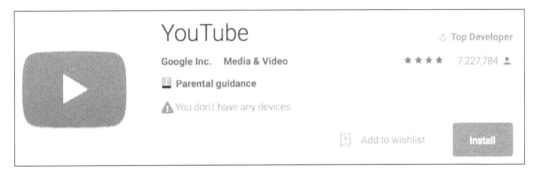

We also need the e-mail, a mobile number, and our website, which is optional. According to Google, it is needed in case someone has to contact us in relation to the content published.

The Google Play Developer console

When we open the publisher account, if we have no apps published, we will see four of the main features of the developer console, as shown in the following image:

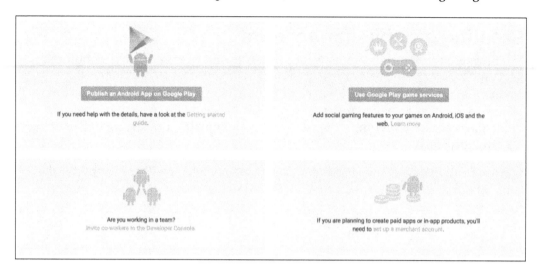

The first option is to publish an Android app, and it is the option we will follow in the book. However, before this, we will describe quickly the other options to keep in mind.

The second option is about the Google Play game services. If you develop a game where you want the players to save and submit their score and have a scores ranking, you will need a server to store these scores and retrieve them, maybe even have a username and a login for the player. The game services do this for us.

It provides an API that is shared across games, linked with the Google account of the user, where we can manage leaderboards and achievements. It even provides the API and infrastructure to implement multiplayer games, both real-time multiplayer and turn-based ones.

The third option, the one at the bottom to the left, is about sharing the developer console. We might want to allow other developers to update an app. This will help, for instance, in the case of a company, where there will be people in charge of setting the name, description, images of the app, and marketing in general and other people in charge of the app upload and the developers. We can configure the access to the console and to a specific application.

INVITE A NEW USER

Email address

Choose a role for this user

Product lead ▼

☑ Create & edit draft apps

☑ Edit store listing, pricing & distribution

☐ Manage Production APKs

☑ Manage Alpha & Beta APKs

☑ Manage Alpha & Beta users

☐ Create apps distributed only to Google Apps domain

☐ Change distribution restriction

☐ View financial reports

☐ Reply to reviews

☑ Edit games

☐ Publish games

[Send Invitation]   Cancel

The fourth and final option is the merchant account; we need this if want to sell paid apps or in-app products. This is an example of the merchant account from a paid app; we can see payments completed and cancelled. If a user purchases our app, he/she has two hours to claim a refund in case he/she didn't like it.

Payments Merchant Center

	● Charged	22-Jun-2015 08:09:08	12999...1373746124131350
Orders	✕ Cancelled	22-Jun-2015 04:31:21	12999...1311175360278315
Payments	● Charged	21-Jun-2015 12:03:13	12999...1360852832805247
Settings	● Charged	20-Jun-2015 02:28:44	12999...1343047272919587

We saw an empty developer console with the four main options because we didn't have an app published yet; if we had apps published, this is what we would see. The **Publish** button is at the top in this case:

On the initial screen, we can see the different apps, whether they are free or paid, the active installs, and the total installs. Active installs mean the people that have the app at the moment and that did not uninstall it after downloading. Total installs mean the count of all the times the app was installed.

We can also see the ratings and number of crashes. We can take a look at more details, such as comments from the users and error crash reports, if we click on the app and go into the detail view.

Publishing an app

Continuing with the upload process, when we click on **+ Add** new application, we are asked for a name and a default language. After this, we can choose how to start the process by uploading an APK or preparing the store listing.

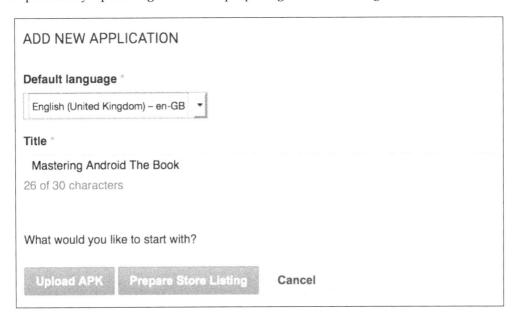

These are two different processes: one is uploading the APK file, and the other is setting the title of the app, a description, an image, if it is paid or free, and so on—all the different options to be shown in Play Store.

Let's start with the uploading of the APK file and the different testing groups.

Uploading the APK file

Remember that when we upload an APK, the package name of our application has to be unique in the Play Store; we can only upload an APK with an existing package name if we want to update an app previously published by us and if the certificate that we used to sign the initial download is the same certificate we used to sign the new APK.

The first things we notice when we click on **upload the APK** are the three different tabs with the names: **Production**, **Beta**, and **Alpha**.

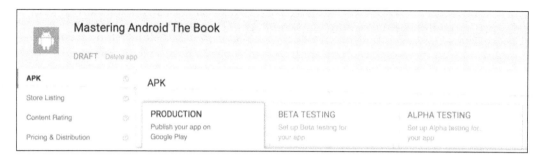

We can release our app in two test groups and in production. Production means that it is published in Play Store; it is public and visible to everyone. For a while, this was the only option available in the developer console until they added the staged rollout.

The staged rollout allows us to release the app to a limited group of users. To select the users, we have different options; we can invite these users by e-mail, share a link, or create a Google group or G+ community, inviting the users to the group and sharing the link of the app with them. Only these users will then see the app in the Play Store. This is useful to get feedback from some users before our app is released to the world and, of course, to prevent bugs and bad reviews of the app in production. We can also select the percentage of users our app is to be published to in production; for instance, if we have a million users, we can release to 10 percent first and double-check that everything is ok before doing a massive release.

We can have different versions of our app in different stages; for instance, we can have version 1.0.0 published, 1.0.1 in beta testing, and 1.0.2 in alpha testing. We can roll out the APK from alpha to beta and from beta to production, but we can't roll back.

The concept that we will now explain is very important. Once we publish a version of our app, we can't go back to a previous published version. It could happen that we have a working version of our app in the Play Store, we develop a new version, it works fine in our device, and we think it is ready to be uploaded. It's Friday afternoon, and we don't bother testing because we think, "Oh, I'm sure it's fine. I just did a small change of two lines, that won't affect anything". We upload version 1.0.4. After a couple of hours, we start receiving crash reports from Play Store. It's the moment of panic; the only thing we can do now is undo the publishing of the current app to prevent more damage and start working on a fix as soon as possible. However, if the fix is not easy, the most sensible thing would be to generate the last known working version again (1.0.3), increase the version number and code to 1.0.5, and upload it to Play Store.

However, this could get worse; if we had a database and the structure changed from 1.0.3 to 1.0.4 and our code is not ready to accept a downgrade of the database from 1.0.4 to 1.0.3 renamed as 1.0.5, we will know that we will be working all weekend, only to be fired on Monday morning. To sum up our point, it is much better to prevent rather than heal; so, use the staged rollout, do all the testing necessary before releasing, and avoid releasing on Friday afternoon just in case.

Preparing the store listing

Preparing the store listing for a developer can be the most boring part, but it needs to be done in order to publish an app; there are some mandatory assets and fields that we can't skip.

First, we need a title for our app, a short description of up to 80 characters and a long description of up to 4000. The title will be the first thing that we see while searching for our app; the short description can be seen, for instance, in tablets while browsing apps. This is the *elevator pitch* of our app, and we need to describe it here in the main function:

The long description will be shown when we go to the detail view of this app. In terms of appearing in more searches and earning visibility, it is good to identify and add keywords related to our app in the description. The use of unrelated keywords to attract downloads is banned from Google, and if you do this, you will receive a warning in the developer console, and your app will need some changes before being approved and published again.

At this point, we have the option to internationalize our app's listing, repeating these three fields mentioned in as many languages as we want, and they will be displayed in different languages automatically, depending on the user's language.

The next step is to develop the graphics, and we need to take screenshots here. Screenshots can easily be taken in your device with a key combination; for instance, in a Samsung Galaxy 3, this is done by pressing the *volume down* and *menu* keys at the same time. They can also be taken from Android Studio by selecting the camera icon in the Android view.

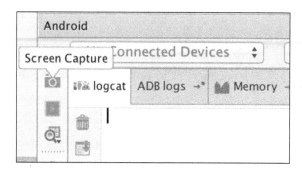

Apart from screenshots, we need a 512 x 512 hi-res icon; this must be the same as or very similar to the icon that we are using for our app in the uploaded version, otherwise it will throw a warning. For this reason, it's good to create the icon in 512 x 512 always and then scale it down to use in our app. The other way around will result in a scaled up image with bad quality. This is an example of where the icon is displayed:

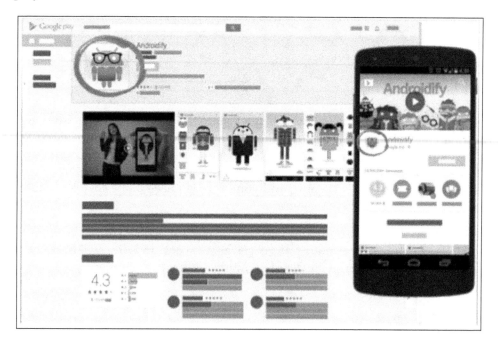

The last image we need is the feature graphic. This is a 1024 x 500 graphic that shows the features of our app. This is the graphic that will be shown in our app featured on Google Play. It will be shown in the Play Store app; if we have a promo video, the feature graphic will still be shown while the video is not playing.

We need to continue with categorization; depending on whether our app is a game or an application, we need to choose different categories. If you are not sure about which category to choose, take a look in Play Store for apps similar to yours.

After this, we need to select the content rating; starting in May 2015, every app needs to have the new rating system. According to Google, this new content rating provides an easy way to communicate familiar and locally relevant content ratings to your users and helps improve app engagement by targeting the right audience for your content as seen in `https://support.google.com/googleplay/android-developer/answer/188189`.

Our contact details are automatically completed, so the last thing we need to do is accept the privacy policy, and then we can click on **Pricing & Distribution**.

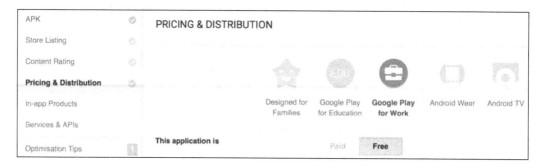

This is where we make our app free or paid; this step can't be reverted. If the app is a paid one, we can set a price, and Google will convert it to different currencies in different countries; although, we can set different prices for each country. We can opt into different developer groups; for instance, if we develop an app for kids, we can include it in **designed for families**. This will increase our chances to be highlighted in kids' sections and distributed for third-party networks related with kids' apps.

In this section, we can select the countries were we want our app to be distributed as well. This can be used as well as a staged releasing strategy the first the time the app is published.

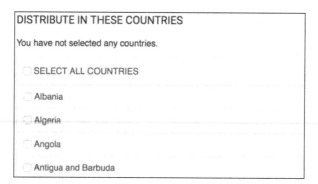

Completing all of the above, we will be able to publish our app by clicking on **Publish** in the upper right corner.

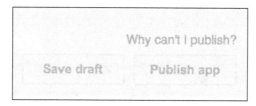

If the button is disabled, you can click on **Why can't I publish?**, and it will list the requirements on the left-hand side. Once the app is published, it can take a couple of hours to appear in the Play Store. The easiest way to find out whether the app is published yet is to navigate to our app using the package name in the URL. In our case, the URL would be, `https://play.google.com/store/apps/details?id=com.packtpub.masteringandroidapp`.

This is it! We have completed the book from the beginners' to a more advanced level with enough knowledge to upload an app well-designed and built that is backward-compatible and monetized.

We wish you success with your apps and we hope you make the next Angry Birds or the next WhatsApp!

Thanks a lot for purchasing and finishing this book. For suggestions, improvements, or any feedback, don't hesitate to contact me at `Antonio@suitapps.com` or follow me on Twitter at `@AntPachon`.

Summary

In this final chapter of the book, we started learning how to create different builds of our applications, combining build types with product flavors to obtain build variants.

After that, we learned how to monetize our app, adding different types of adverts and explaining the key points of advertisement monetization.

We also exported the app, obfuscated and signed with a release certificate, from Android Studio and from the command line using Gradle.

To finish, we uploaded and published our app in Play Store.

Index

H

handlers 61, 62

I

images
  downloading 126
  downloading, traditional way 126-130
  downloading, with Volley 131-133
  mastering 134
  vector drawables 134, 135
integration test
  Espresso, configuring 227
  running 231
  with Espresso 226
  writing 228-230

J

J2EE (Java 2 Enterprise Edition) 153
JSON 53, 54

L

leaks
  detecting 139-141
  locating 139-141
  preventing 142
leaks, preventing
  activity references 142
  context references 142
  WeakReference, using 142, 143
lists
  about 76
  custom Adapter, creating 81-87
  ListViews using, built-in views used 77-80
  ViewHolder pattern, applying 89-92
  views, recycling 88
loaders 65
logs
  about 218
  working with 218, 219

M

map
  adding 207
  fragment, adding 207-209
  fragment, implementing 210
marker
  adding 212
  data, retrieving from Parse 212
  displaying, for each location 213, 214
  title, adding to mark 215
MasteringAndroidApp
  creating 9, 10
material design
  about 2-4
  URL 16
memory management
  about 139
  leaks, detecting 139-141
  leaks, locating 139-141
  leaks, preventing 142
monetization
  about 243
  advertisement model 244
  freemium model 244
MonkeyTalk
  used, for recording UI tests 234, 235
motion
  adding, CoordinatorLayout used 117-122

N

nine patch 137, 138
NotificationCompat
  URL 193
  using 192, 193

O

observer pattern 70-72
OkHttp 49, 52

U

UI tests
  about 232
  recording, MonkeyTalk used 234
Up navigation 122, 123

V

vector drawables 134, 135
ViewHolder pattern
  applying 89-92
ViewPager
  about 27
  adapter 27-29
  tabs, customizing 30
  tabs, sliding 29, 30
views
  recycling 88
Volley
  used, for downloading images 131-133

W

WeakReference
  using 142, 143

Thank you for buying
Mastering Android Application Development

About Packt Publishing

Packt, pronounced 'packed', published its first book, *Mastering phpMyAdmin for Effective MySQL Management*, in April 2004, and subsequently continued to specialize in publishing highly focused books on specific technologies and solutions.

Our books and publications share the experiences of your fellow IT professionals in adapting and customizing today's systems, applications, and frameworks. Our solution-based books give you the knowledge and power to customize the software and technologies you're using to get the job done. Packt books are more specific and less general than the IT books you have seen in the past. Our unique business model allows us to bring you more focused information, giving you more of what you need to know, and less of what you don't.

Packt is a modern yet unique publishing company that focuses on producing quality, cutting-edge books for communities of developers, administrators, and newbies alike. For more information, please visit our website at www.packtpub.com.

About Packt Open Source

In 2010, Packt launched two new brands, Packt Open Source and Packt Enterprise, in order to continue its focus on specialization. This book is part of the Packt Open Source brand, home to books published on software built around open source licenses, and offering information to anybody from advanced developers to budding web designers. The Open Source brand also runs Packt's Open Source Royalty Scheme, by which Packt gives a royalty to each open source project about whose software a book is sold.

Writing for Packt

We welcome all inquiries from people who are interested in authoring. Book proposals should be sent to author@packtpub.com. If your book idea is still at an early stage and you would like to discuss it first before writing a formal book proposal, then please contact us; one of our commissioning editors will get in touch with you.

We're not just looking for published authors; if you have strong technical skills but no writing experience, our experienced editors can help you develop a writing career, or simply get some additional reward for your expertise.

Asynchronous Android

ISBN: 978-1-78328-687-4   Paperback: 146 pages

Harness the power of multi-core mobile processors to build responsive Android applications

1. Learn how to use Android's high-level concurrency constructs to keep your applications smooth and responsive.

2. Leverage the full power of multi-core mobile CPUs to get more work done in less time.

3. From quick calculations to scheduled downloads, each chapter explains the available mechanisms of asynchronous programming in detail.

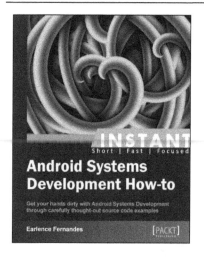

Instant Android Systems Development How-to

ISBN: 978-1-84951-976-2   Paperback: 100 pages

Get your hands dirty with Android Systems Development through carefully thought-out source code examples

1. Learn something new in an Instant! A short, fast, focused guide delivering immediate results.

2. A gentle introduction to Android Platform Internals and how to make changes to the system.

3. Gain the skills necessary for building high quality systems code for the Android Platform.

Please check **www.PacktPub.com** for information on our titles

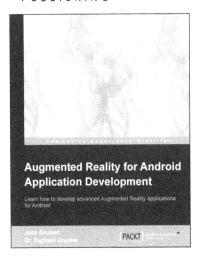

Augmented Reality for Android Application Development

ISBN: 978-1-78216-855-3   Paperback: 130 pages

Learn how to develop advanced Augmented Reality applications for Android

1. Understand the main concepts and architectural components of an AR application.

2. Step-by-step learning through hands-on programming combined with a background of important mathematical concepts.

3. Efficiently and robustly implement some of the main functional AR aspects.

Building Android Games with OpenGL ES [Video]

ISBN: 978-1-78328-613-3   Duration: 01:42 hours

A comprehensive course exploring the creation of beautiful games with OpenGL ES

1. Create captivating games through creating simple and effective codes in Java.

2. Develop a version of the classic game Breakout and see how to monetize it.

3. Step-by-step instructions and theoretical concepts describe each activity before you implement them.

Please check **www.PacktPub.com** for information on our titles